LOCOMOTION PAPERS

The Railways of Purbeck

by
R.W. Kidner

THE OAKWOOD PRESS

© Oakwood Press & R.W. Kidner 2000
British Library Cataloguing in Publication Data
A Record for this book is available from the British Library
ISBN 0 85361 557 8
First published 1973
Reprinted 1976, 1979
Second Edition 1988
Third Edition 2000
Typeset by Oakwood Graphics.
Repro by Ford Graphics, Ringwood, Hants.
Printed by Cambrian Printers, Aberystwyth, Ceredigion.

Author's Note

Of my first visit to Swanage nearly 80 years ago I recall nothing except the great stone globe at Durlston. However on later visits I was able to appreciate the charm of the Southern Railway branch, the green livery of the Swanage 'T1' class kept spotless by a friendly staff. Later still, excursions across the heaths brought realisation that there was much more of railway interest in the 'Island'; the Furzebrook china clay workers on their way home in their riding wagon, jumping off at the main road to work the catchpoint and stopblock without actually halting fascinated me.

Because of the war I did not visit between 1938 and 1949 and thus missed the change of gauge at Norden and the last days of Fayle's Lewin engine. However, later the convenient caravan site at Smedmore House allowed more exploration, and a sight of the new Swanage Railway beginning its life in the 1970s.

Few photographers penetrated Purbeck until the 1930s; there is only one known photograph of a train on the branch in its first 25 years, no coverage at all of the Newton clay operations or of the shale extraction at Kimmeridge. However, study of early maps gives important clues to industrial history, and timetables show how Swanage was progressively given the train services it deserved. That the town may finally be served again by a rail connection to London is a bonus many others have not enjoyed.

R.W. Kidner
2000

Title page: A 'Q' class 0-6-0 hauls a down goods over the Studland Road at Corfe in July 1955. The low ground at far left was worked by Fayles for clay early in the century.
J.R. Bonsor

Front cover: An early colour photograph of *Secundus*, the Bellis & Seekings-built 0-6-0T of 1874. She is seen here on the Pike Bros Tramway in September 1948.
Pendragon Collection/Colour-Rail

Rear cover, top: BR Standard 2-6-4T No. 80146 is seen entering Swanage on 4th June, 1966.
R.C. Riley

Rear cover, bottom: A narrow gauge clay train at Norden on 19th June, 1970.   *R.C. Riley*

Published by The Oakwood Press (Usk), P.O. Box 13, Usk, Mon., NP15 1YS.
E-mail: oakwood-press@dial.pipex.com
Website: www.oakwood-press.dial.pipex.com

Contents

'T1' class 0-4-4T No. E70 takes water at Swanage on Sunday 7th August, 1932 for the 4.30 pm, the first train out on a Sunday. The old coach body for enginemen behind the shed has been replaced by a hut.   *Author*

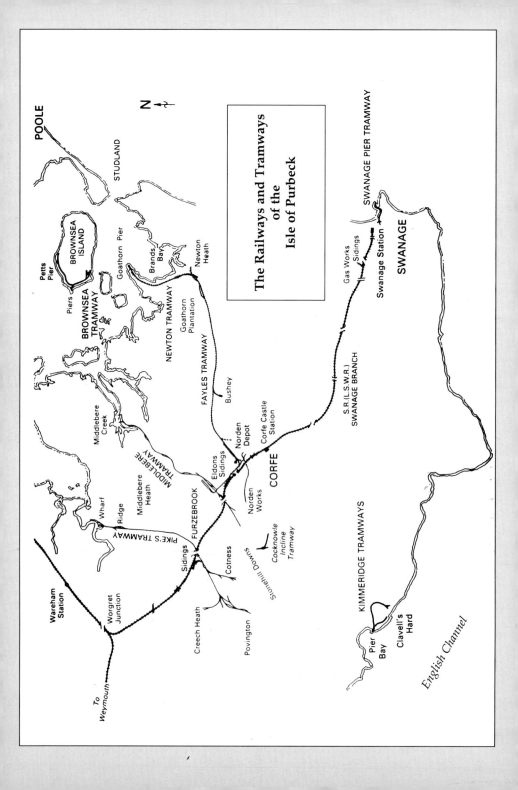

N

POOLE

STUDLAND

Petts
Pier

Piers

BROWNSEA
ISLAND

BROWNSEA
TRAMWAY

Goathorn Pier

Brands
Bay

Newton
Heath

NEWTON TRAMWAY

Goathorn
Plantation

FAYLES TRAMWAY

Bushey

Middlebere
Creek

Wharf

Ridge

MIDDLEBERE TRAMWAY

Middlebere
Heath

PIKE'S TRAMWAY

FURZEBROOK

Sidings

Eldons
Sidings

Norden
Depot

Corfe Castle
Station

CORFE

Norden
Works

Cocknowle
Incline
Tramway

Stonehill Downs

Cotness

Wareham
Station

Worget
Junction

Creech Heath

Povington

To
Weymouth

SWANAGE PIER TRAMWAY

Gas Works
Sidings

Swanage Station

SWANAGE

S.R. (L.S.W.R.)
SWANAGE BRANCH

KIMMERIDGE TRAMWAYS

Pier
Bay

Clavell's
Hard

English Channel

The Railways and Tramways of the Isle of Purbeck

Chapter One

The Swanage Branch, LSWR

The 'Isle' of Purbeck comprises a promontory extending some ten miles south-west of the River Frome at Wareham, being bounded on the north by the river and on the north-east by the ramifications of Poole Harbour, a mass of winding channels through which in ancient days this area was approached, before other means of communication existed. The 'island' is bisected by a ridge of hills running east to west through Corfe, and it is the combination of limestone plateau, clay vale, and chalk ridges which gives this small area such a variety and interest. The clay vale was settled in mesolithic times, certainly before 3500 BC, and by the 12th century working of a local stone, and of the scarce material known as 'Purbeck Marble', had begun, being used in various cathedrals, including Salisbury and Exeter, and in Westminster Abbey. Stone workings were mostly in the area near North Swanage, Langton, and Worth Matravers, and the stone seems to have been taken along narrow tracks to the nearest navigable creeks in Poole Harbour, and later to Swanage Bay.

There were several ancient little ports along the southern margin of Poole Harbour, which forms the north shore of Purbeck: Wytch, Corfe, Russell Quay, Middlebere Creek - all were on relatively deep channels leading into the main channel for seaborne traffic running into the port of Poole. That this formed a satisfactory method of transport is proved by the fact that in Purbeck, unlike many other mining areas, the main line railway when it came did not immediately draw on to itself the traffic from the mines.

About 100 years ago, the holiday 'industry' began to assume importance; the fishing village of Swanage with its improvised methods of shipping stone had given way to a small Victorian town. All the trappings of Victorian holiday-making began to appear - and there can be few seaside towns with more masonic knick-knacks - so that by the end of World War I, when family holidays became general and not the prerequisite of the upper-middle class, the town was ready to boom.

However, in the years immediately following Queen Victoria's accession the targets aimed at by the newly-born railways were limited. It was a new-fangled thing, which had not yet proved itself. On the south coast, there were three places which three separate companies set out to reach: Dover, Brighton and Southampton. The first train from London to Southampton ran in 1840, a year ahead of the Brighton line and four years ahead of Dover. Further west there lay whole counties waiting to be opened up. The Great Western's great sweep to the West was making progress, but well to the north, and when the London & Southampton Railway became the London & South Western (LSWR), the opening up of Hampshire and Dorset was very much in its mind. The Southampton & Dorchester Railway, promoted locally, came under the wing of the LSWR, and was opened on 1st June, 1847, though it was not available to London trains until 29th July, as junctions at Southampton were uncompleted.

This map of Swanage shows the position of the proposed LSWR station. A dotted line representing a Tramway has been added from the Pier Tramway to the new station; this was not built, but a standard gauge LSWR tramway was built on somewhat the same line. The terminus (as built) did not extend quite so far towards the front as shown here.

A wayside station on this line was set up at Wareham, well outside the town, as the citizens had followed the lead of the New Forest Commissioners in refusing to have any actual contact with the sordid reality of railways. The line was then single, and remained something of a backwater as the LSWR strove to reach the far west by another route, through Salisbury. However, in 1857 the LSWR ran into Weymouth (over Great Western metals), and during 1863 the line from Wimborne through to Dorchester was doubled.

Various attempts were made to promote a branch line from Wareham either to Swanage or to the clay workings. One line, the Isle of Purbeck Railway, succeeded in getting an Act in 1863, but backed down in face of local hostility. However, the town of Swanage was growing rapidly, and could not indefinitely be without modern transport. When the Swanage Railway was promoted and received its Act (44-45 Vict. cap. 159)* in 1881, the moment of truth had arrived. The problem for the Wareham worthies was a real one; because they had insisted on the siting of Wareham station north of the town, which had now grown out to it, a direct branch to Swanage would cut the town in half. A Solomon's judgement was produced; the branch would start at Worgret, 1¼ miles to the west, and not pass through Wareham at all. Worgret was a lonely and remote cluster of houses, which would not have had much say in the matter, and did not even rate a station at the junction. On the other hand, Wareham station was too cramped to handle the branch traffic, and plans were drawn up for a larger station on the other side of the level crossing. And so for the whole of its life the Swanage branch was worked as if it started at Wareham, but its trains ran the first 1¼ miles on the main line to Weymouth.

The railway duly opened on 20th May, 1885. From its inception it was worked by the LSWR, and by an Act of 1886 (49-50 Vict. cap. 110) the Swanage Railway was absorbed into the larger company.

A description of the line would be fitting here. As stated, the branch left the Weymouth line at Worgret; here there was a passing loop south of the junction, so that a train from Swanage could await a path on the up line to Wareham without fouling a down branch train. Worgret Junction box (126 miles from Waterloo) was a busy place in the summer, and also hard work. When in the 1930s the *Southern Railway Magazine* was trying to find the longest signalman's pull, Worgret claimed on three counts: Swanage branch up distant 1,406 yds, down main distant 1,532 yds, up main distant 1,680 yds - it did not win however. The branch became single on leaving the loop, crossing the streams of the Frome and various bits of marsh, with a gradient of 1 in 78 to Creech to run over Grange and Creech Heaths. The latter was already occupied by the Pike Brothers' clay workings, and the LSWR crossed over their line from Ridge near Furzebrook House; no exchange siding seems to have been put in at that time. A mile and a quarter further on, passing under the Wareham-Corfe Road at milepost 130, the branch met the ancient Middlebere Plateway (Fayle's), and made a narrow tunnel through its embankment to accommodate it, though it seems the pits west of the line may have been more or less worked out. The new line from the Middlebere Plateway to pits to the south-east ran parallel with the LSWR. Here the single-line Eldon's siding was placed for clay transfer. The new Fayle's line crossed the LSWR either at opening or shortly after.

* The original Act had also given powers for a railway or tramway from Swanage station to the stone 'bankers' on the front, and this is described later.

ACT

To Incorporate a Company for the Construction of the Swanage Railway and for other purposes.

[*Royal Assent, 18th July, 1881.*]

WHEREAS the construction of Railways to connect Swanage Preamble. with the London and South Western Railway near Wareham all in the county of Dorset would be of public and local advantage:

5   And whereas the persons in this Act named are willing with others at their own expense to construct such Railways and are desirous of being incorporated into a Company for the purpose:

And whereas plans and sections of the said Railways showing the lines and levels thereof with a book of reference to the plans 10 containing the names of the owners and lessees or reputed owners and lessees and of the occupiers of the lands through which the

The front page of the 1881 Act for the Swanage Railway.

An early photograph of Swanage station, with a train of four-wheeled carriages hauled by a Beattie 2-4-0WT No. 209. Often described as the 'first train', this is unlikely as there are no members of the public present. It appears the station had a staff of at least eight.

Southern Railway

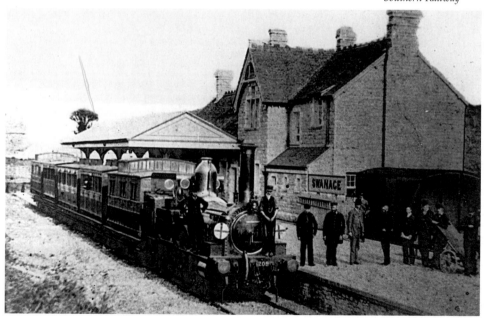

Continuing towards Corfe, it becomes clear that there was no choice of route; it had to be between the high hill on which the castle stands and the equally high East Hill. The road was already there, and the branch, after passing over a magnificent four-arch stone viaduct, had to do some cutting before entering Corfe Castle station (131 m). This is in excellent taste and fits well with the castle and other stone buildings of the village. There was a passing loop and a long and a short siding. The heath now begins again, as the line finds it way down to sea level, with gradients as steep as 1 in 77. It entered the town, when first built, on the north side of what little development had taken place (it was now running west to east, rather than south), and little demolition can have been required. There was a siding with points facing Wareham 150 yds west of the Victoria Avenue bridge, to serve the gasworks. As the branch completed its last steep down gradient, a two-line siding protected by a gate, for stone traffic, could be seen on the right, though this is unlikely to have been there at the time of opening. The 136¼ m. post was on the station platform.

The gasworks siding, which had a reception line on the 1 in 110 grade, branched to the east; at 130 yds a point divided it, the left-hand line going on to a turntable which gave access to the retort house; the right-hand line ran to a siding for the Worth Quarries (later Swanworth Quarries). The stone siding adjacent to the road bridge was the property of W. Haysom & Sons. A further stone firm, Beavis, had a part of a siding and a crane at the south end of the station layout; this could perhaps have been a relic of the former tramway to the stone 'bankers' mentioned later.

The town the LSWR was arriving to serve was still small, the development being only from the Royal Victoria Hotel up to Northbrook Road. East of Mowlem Institute there was nothing but some stone bankers not served by the pier tramway, and a few bathing machines at the end of Victoria Avenue (then called Mowlem Road). However, growth was rapid for the next 20 years when it largely ceased until after World War II. The Ward Lock guide for 1934 put it well, 'a dear inconsequential little town, with all sorts of lovable absurdities in the way of lamp posts, clock towers . . . bestowed during the 19th century by citizens who loved it . . .'

Although the station building at Swanage is neat and small, the layout was unusually large. A trailing point led into an attractive one-engine locomotive shed, with turntable. Then another long quadruple siding ran off to the right before the line passed under a road bridge to enter the station proper. The locomotive shed was built at an angle which made it impossible to run from the station straight across the table and into the shed - so some muscle was required in the morning even for a tank engine. The station had two platforms, that on the south side being even shorter than the main one. It was about equidistant from the Parade and the High Street and therefore well-sited. All mileposts on the branch were numbered from Waterloo; bridge numbers ran from 1 near Worgret box to 31, the overbridge by the turntable at Swanage.

Originally one of the sidings to the south of the station was extended by a tramway running in a narrow alley behind the shops in Station Road, to a turntable on a cross-siding carrying a crane and. serving a stone store. This was very close to the stone store on the Pier Tramway on the south side of Institute

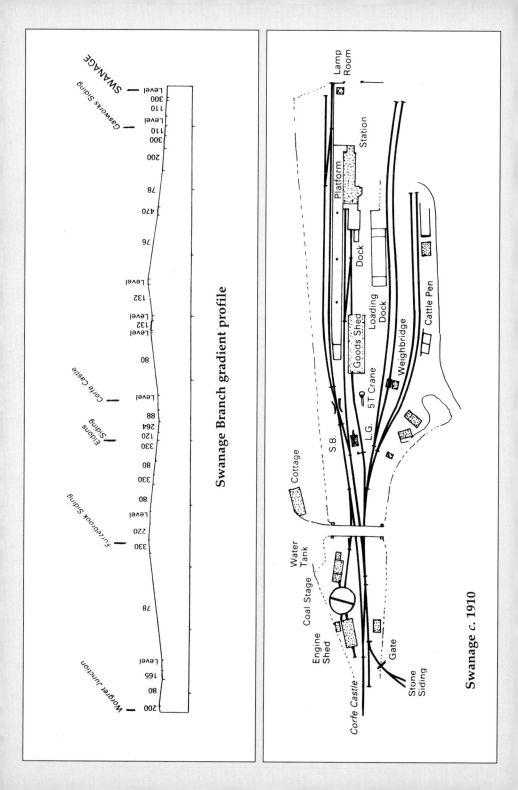

Swanage Branch gradient profile

Swanage *c.* 1910

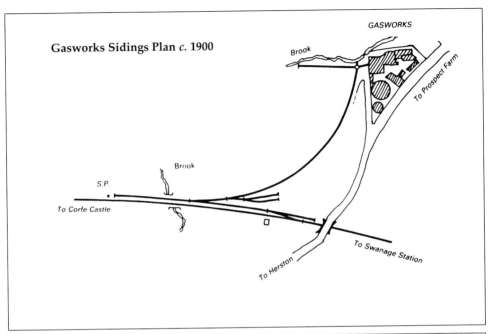

Gasworks Sidings Plan *c.* **1900**

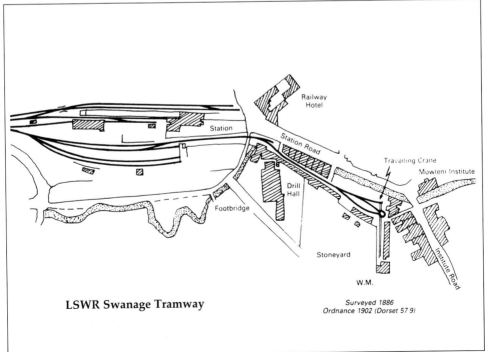

LSWR Swanage Tramway

Surveyed 1886
Ordnance 1902 (Dorset 57 9)

Corfe Castle from the Station 1956.

A through train from Bournemouth hauled by '460' class 4-4-0 No. 477 approaches Corfe Castle station about 1906. This postcard view was published by J. Welch & Sons, Portsmouth.

Road, but of course the lines were of differing gauge. The LSWR tramway was still on the 1906 Ordnance Survey map, but must have closed about that time due to road development south of the station.

The service at opening was modest and inexpensive. The line was worked on the 'one engine in steam' basis; the engine left Swanage with the first train at 7.20 am; there were five trains each way and a mid-day goods; the last train left Wareham at 9.10 pm and the engine returned to its shed. From 1st August, 1885 the goods working was a 'mixed' train (i.e. carrying passengers if required); it took 45 minutes. It must be remembered that there was no clay wagon pick-up work to do as Eldon and Furzebrook sidings did not exist, so this timing, which was 18 minutes longer than the passenger timing, only took into account shunting duties at Corfe, and probably an allowance for a bit of crawling up the banks if there was some heavy coal or stone in the train. There was no Sunday service.

Over the years the service was somewhat improved, and through workings in the summer period increased. It is not possible to say exactly when through coaches from Waterloo commenced, as *Bradshaw* did not make a clear enough distinction between through coaches and connections. In 1922 the 'Pines Express', which travelled via the Somerset & Dorset Joint Railway (S&DJR), carried a through coach from Manchester to Swanage. The branch train in the down bay could leave as soon as the Weymouth train had cleared the section to Worgret; if there was a through coach the gap in the timetable might be longer, as the branch train would have to back into the through platform to pick it up. In 1931 (Winter service) there were 13 down trains on the branch; trains leaving Waterloo at 12.30 pm and the 4.30 pm and 6.30 pm had good Swanage connections or through coaches; the 4.30 pm from Bournemouth Central ran through to Swanage, with no connection to Weymouth at Wareham. The connection from the 4.30 ex-Waterloo left Wareham at 7.17 pm and was followed at 7.47 by a connection off the Bournemouth West to Dorchester train - there were examples in various years of two trains following each other over the branch; the second train passed the first one returning at Corfe Castle. The Sunday service was meagre - two trains, both in late afternoon; in the morning no wheel turned to distract the inhabitants from their church-going. In the up direction there were also 13 trains, the 9.50 am, 1.23 pm and 5.27 pm being the London trains. The 7.50 pm was a through train to Bournemouth, running fast from Wareham apart from a stop at Poole. If anyone for London was unwise enough to wait for the last train, the 8.45 pm, they arrived at Waterloo at four in the morning. This connection from Wareham was typical of the timetabling mania of the day: on Saturdays it did not call at Holton Heath or Branksome, it only called at Sway on Wednesdays and Saturdays, and it called at New Milton only to set down.

The LSWR was in a monopoly position in Swanage, unlike the situation in Bournemouth or Weymouth; however it was not complete. The steamers from Bournemouth which had served the town before the coming of the railway continued to run, latterly only in summer. Then there was the bus; one guide book in the 1930s suggested that people from the Midlands and North might prefer to travel by the S&DJR to Poole and take the bus to Swanage. However,

In this busy scene at Swanage c. 1910 'A12' class 0-4-2 No. 607 is bringing in a long train of six-wheeled carriages, while a set of bogie stock is parked on the long head-shunt; the branch 4-4-2T is taking water.

Lens of Sutton

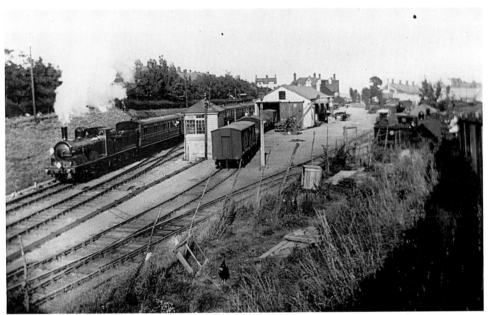

A view of the station at Swanage about 1914, with an 'A12' class 0-4-2 taking out a through train to London of corridor stock. *Lens of Sutton*

Another view from the bridge; a different 'A12' (with Drummond boiler) is on the left, while a '302' class 0-6-0 shunts the sidings. *Lens of Sutton*

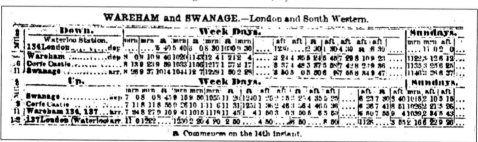

The branch passenger timetable for April 1910.

Passenger timetable for July 1922.

The branch train waiting to leave Wareham about 1910 behind Adams 'Radial' 4-4-2T No. 133;
a postcard view by M.J. Ridley of Boscombe.   *Author's Collection*

this was a tedious journey as it led across the Sandbanks chain-ferry; owing to the steep approach to the ramp, buses had to have their rear ends cut away to avoid grounding on the beach. The S&DJR ran up to five through trains from the North to Bournemouth and Poole, and in some years there was a through carriage for Swanage; with a change at Poole the journey by this route from Birmingham to Swanage then took well under six hours and was a good deal more convenient than travelling through London.

In the years before World War I the resorts between Bournemouth and Weymouth were regarded as important enough for people from the North to have convenient trains to them. This was a time when a few coaches, sometimes only one, would be passed between companies to avoid passengers having to change trains. In the 1910 tables the London & North Western Railway provided trains leaving Liverpool at 10.00 am and Manchester at 10.10 which had through coaches to Bournemouth, allowing a Swanage arrival at 7.14 pm.

The Great Northern Railway cited the 8.00 am from Newcastle as arriving at Kings Cross to connect with a through train to Bournemouth and Weymouth; there was also a through train starting at York making its way to Bournemouth via the Great Central. The Midland also by way of its part-owned Somerset & Dorset Railway sent down many trains; the 11.00 am from Derby via Templecombe and Blandford provided a switch at Poole which would land a passenger at Swanage by 5.17 pm.

The local service remained infrequent; however a late train was added on Thursdays which left Swanage at 9.45 pm and returned from Wareham at 12.14 am. Next year there were some additions, including the 12.40 pm from Waterloo being shown as non-stop to Swanage in 3 hours 10 minutes.

In one way the branch was unfortunate. When the LSWR began its halt-building programme in 1903 one might have expected one or two in Purbeck. But to be truthful, there was nothing to 'halt' at. Owing partly to geography but mainly to the conservative attitude of landowners, notably the Bankes family, no holiday villages ever developed in the peninsular.

At Wareham on 13th August, 1932; in the down platform the Swanage carriages at the rear of the Weymouth train will be left in the platform; the branch train from Swanage entering will not be able to handle the through coaches, which have their own engine waiting.   *Author*

The Swanage portion (Ironclad stock) being attached to a London train from Weymouth at Wareham on 13th August, 1932. The operation is controlled from the ground frame on the right.
Author

Chapter Two

Southern Railway and British Rail

The 1930s were perhaps the best years for the Swanage branch. Holiday traffic was increasing fast, and private cars had not yet made great inroads. In addition, the area had always been a favoured one for Territorial Army camps - so much heath and down to put tents on - and with the increasing likelihood of war, these were also increasing. The limit for troop trains seem to have been 10 coaches plus extras (horse-boxes, field kitchens, sometimes guns) and these trains took some starting up the bank out of Swanage. Western Section engines in those days carried their power classification letter on the front-end of the running plate. A small Drummond 4-4-0 classified 'F' and an Adams 4-4-0 classified 'I' double-heading a full train seemed to get away fairly well; another train headed by two 'M7' 0-4-4Ts (classified 'K') did, as expected, have a hard struggle. It was particularly difficult if the main train had to set back after leaving the platform to pick up baggage vehicles from the goods yard, as it gave no space for a run at the bank. The type of engine which could be stabled at Swanage was of course limited by the length of the 50 ft turntable. From photographs, it would appear that some time after 1938 an entry was made into the engine shed from the Wareham end, thus enabling an engine too long or heavy for the turntable to use the shed facilities.

The war did not greatly affect the branch; for several reasons this part of the coast was not a very attractive invasion choice, however the 14th Super Heavy Battery, 5th Corps, set up rail-mounted long-range guns on short spur lines, one 300 yds on the Swanage side of Furzebrook, another ½ mile the other side (about October 1940) and they stayed for some 10 months. The SR provided 'K10' class 4-4-0 No. 393 to service them.

The whole area around Poole Harbour became a restricted area, and the creeks of the Wareham Channel became familiar with Navy MTBs. Tank exercises were held east of Kimmeridge and 1½ miles of light rails were laid at Swalland Farm for target practice on moving objects.

The passenger service on the branch was maintained at seven trains per day; the 6.36 am down from Wareham passed the 6.23 up in the Worgret loop. The late evening train arriving at Wareham at 9.20 pm did not return, and the first train of the day came from Bournemouth. However an engine must have been shedded at Swanage, as the 7.15 up train was followed by a 7.25 up train if one can believe *Bradshaw*. It took exactly 10 minutes for a train from Swanage to clear the section at Corfe Castle.

Afterwards, petrol rationing brought a short term benefit to the passenger traffic, but although visitors to Swanage itself were to increase by leaps and bounds, the railway began a gradual decline, particularly in terms of through trains.

In 1951 the newly created train 'The Royal Wessex' appeared, a short-lived return to the old days of named trains on the former Southern. This was a triple-portion train, with five coaches for Weymouth in front, then two coaches for Swanage, and six coaches for Bournemouth at the rear. It left Waterloo at 4.35 pm and the two coaches arrived in Swanage at 7.52, having been detached from the Weymouth train at Wareham and attached at the rear of the branch push-and-pull; normally the

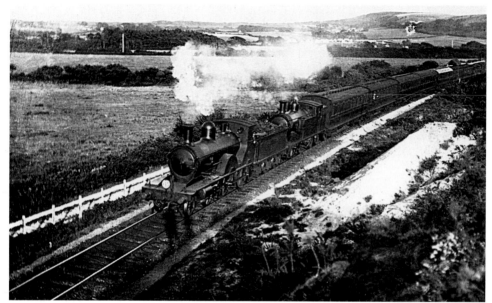

'X6' class 4-4-0 No. 657 and an 'M7' class 0-4-4T haul this evening up through train near Furzebrook on 10th August, 1932.   *Author*

Wareham train leaving Swanage on 15th August, 1932, with a 'T1' class 0-4-4T heading a train comprising the branch set and an extra coach for the summer.   *Author*

Two 'M7' class 0-4-4Ts head a train laid on for the 4th Gloucesters Territorials out of Swanage on 11th August, 1932. Nine corridor coaches, two vans, and two flats of field kitchens formed a daunting load with the gradient starting immediately. *Author*

The alternative to the railway; the paddle steamer *Monarch* from Poole approaches Swanage New Pier in 1934. *Author*

The Corfe Gap and the viaduct across the Studland Road on 11th August, 1934. The up troop train made up from early LSWR bogie stock, plus several vans, is hauled by 'K10' class 4-4-0 No. 387 and one of Adams' 7 ft classes.   *Author*

A goods and empty stock train near Norden in August 1938, with 'T1' 0-4-4T No. 2. On the left Fayles' engine is shunting a weathering bed.   *Author*

Corfe Castle station from the end of the down platform about 1935.   *Lens of Sutton*

Two-coach push-pull sets worked all local trains from the mid-1930s, the 'M7' class engines being fitted with Westinghouse pumps at the off side of the smokebox.   *Lens of Sutton*

SWANAGE BRANCH.

Name of siding.	Position.	(1) Station in charge of working. (2) wagons labelled to †	Gradient at point of connection (1 in)	Catch points provied in sidings at.	Points of siding controlled by or worked from.	If gates provided across siding		Worked by.	Remarks.
						Key to be obtained from.	Key to be returned to.		
Pike's Furzebrook	Up side between Worgret Jct. and Corfe Castle	Corfe Castle	330 falling towards Worgret Jct.	Outgoing ground signal	Ground frame Train Tablet	Corfe Castle		Various goods services	*
Eldon's	Down side between Worgret Jct. and Corfe Castle	Corfe Castle	330 falling towards Corfe Castle	Clearance point	Ground frame Train Tablet	Interlocked by siding points		Various goods services	*
Beevis	Up side Swanage	Swanage	270 falling towards Swanage	—	Extension of goods yard	—	—	—	For working instructions see page 45.
Hayom & Sons	Up side Swanage, Corfe Castle end •	Swanage	90 falling towards Corfe Castle	—	Hand points from siding	Secured by bolt from Swanage box		Shunting engine	For working instructions see page 45. *
Swanage Gas Works	Down side between Corfe Castle and Swanage	Swanage	110 falling towards Swanage	In reception siding about 50 yards from running line	Ground frame Train Tablet	Swanage box		Special services	For working instructions see page 46. *

The Swanage branch listing sidings in the Southern Railway Working Timetable Appendices (Western Section) for 1934.

SWANAGE.

Beavis' siding.—A 10-ton Portland crane has been provided at a spot situated 30 to 40 feet south of the siding extension, and in connection with the movement of wagons to and from the extension, the special attention of the staff engaged in shunting operations is drawn to Rule 112 (a).

Haysom & Sons' sidings.—These sidings (two), which are laid in partly on private property, consist of a main siding which connects with the Railway Company's siding on the up side at Corfe Castle end of Swanage station, and a spur siding connecting, inside the boundary gate, with the main siding, about 50 yards from the points of the Railway Company's siding.

Wagons containing goods consigned to or from Messrs. Haysom & Sons, and empty wagons for their use, may be placed in or taken from the sidings as required, by arrangement with the Station Master at Swanage, such vehicles to be placed immediately inside the gate, or accepted from that point, as the case may be.

Before wagons are placed in the sidings or taken therefrom, there must be an understanding with the staff of the Stone Company that everything is in readiness for such operations to commence.

Swanage Gas Works siding.—Hand points exist in the reception siding at about 130 yards from the point of connection with the running line, and these points control the entrance to a short lead which divides into two parallel private sidings at a point near the Company's boundary by means of a further set of hand points.

The left-hand siding (going in) is used by the Swanage Gas Company and a turntable is situated thereon at about 100 yards from the siding gate, which turntable connects with a short siding leading to the Gas Company's retort house.

The right-hand siding (going in) is used by the Worth Quarries Company and a loading dock is situated approximately 120 yards from the siding gate.

Wagons for the sidings must be hauled from Swanage with a brake van at the rear in which a competent man must ride.

Upon arrival at the siding the tablet must be obtained from the Driver and the ground frame and siding gate opened. The whole train must then be drawn into the reception siding.

Traffic to and from the Gas Works siding must be exchanged between the boundary gate and the turntable, and traffic to and from the Worth Quarries siding must be exchanged immediately inside the siding gate clear of the fouling point.

The special trip must then return to Swanage by means of a propelling movement with the brake van as the leading vehicle in which the competent man must ride.

During the time traffic is being worked to and from the siding, the Corfe Castle and Swanage section must not be fouled by shunting operations at Swanage.

Extracts from the Southern Railway Working Timetable Appendices (Western Section) for 1934.

Station	Turntables (Length of Rail)		Cranes or runways to lift				Weighbridges			High-way vehicle docks	Water columns	
	Engine	Wagon	Outside		Inside		Truck		Cart		No.	Where situated
				Ht. of lift		Ht. of lift	Capa-city	Lth. in	Capa-city			
	ft. ins.	ft. ins.	T. cwts.	ft. ins.	cwts.	ft. ins.	Tons	ft.	Tons			
SWANAGE BRANCH.												
Corfe Castle ...	—	—	---	---	30	10 3	---	---	---	1	—	
Swanage ...	50 0	—	5 0B	17 3	30	11 6	20	14	---	1	1	Loco siding
			3 10A	19 9								

Corfe Castle track plan c. 1950

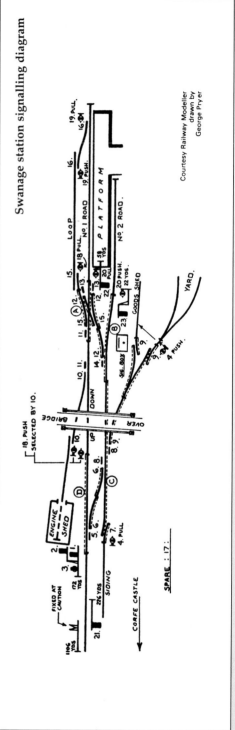

Swanage station signalling diagram

Courtesy Railway Modeller
drawn by
George Pryer

branch train drew forward from the south bay and backed onto the through coaches in the down through platform. The return working was 7.38 am from Swanage.

In 1955 the service from London to Swanage was reasonable and comprised:

Waterloo	1.14 *am*	Swanage	6.48 *am*	via Salisbury, 3rd class
Waterloo	2.40	Swanage	8.40	3rd class, ½ hr wait at Wareham
Waterloo	5.40	Swanage	10.09	
Waterloo	8.30	Swanage	12.19 *pm*	
Waterloo	10.30	Swanage	1.54	Through carriages
Waterloo	11.30	Swanage	3.59	Not Sats
Waterloo	12.30 *pm*	Swanage	3.59	'Bournemouth Belle' to Central
Waterloo	12.35	Swanage	3.59	Sats only
Waterloo	1.30	Swanage	5.21	
Waterloo	3.20	Swanage	6.49	
Waterloo	4.35	Swanage	7.52	'Royal Wessex'; through carriages
Waterloo	6.30	Swanage	9.42	Through carriages

There were four other arrivals at Swanage: 8.53 am from Wareham, 12.38 pm with connection from Southampton, 2.38 pm from Wareham only, and 6 pm from Bournemouth.

In the early 1960s there was one through coach for Swanage in the winter service, normally formed as the fifth coach of a 13-coach train from Waterloo. At Bournemouth Central the rear eight coaches would be removed, and at Wareham the fifth coach would be left in the platform, to be picked up by the push-pull train for Swanage.

The 'Pines Express' was shown in *Bradshaw* as connecting for Swanage. Times were not very exciting: 11 hours from Bradford, 8 hours 36 mins from Manchester, 6 hours 11 mins from Birmingham; but for holidaymakers with large families it was still worth while to avoid the change in London, the change at Poole being a good deal easier. These timings had been made worse as against pre-war ones by arranging a 40 minute wait at Poole and another of 10 minutes at Wareham.

After 'dieselisation' in 1966 the service was altered to allow only one dmu to be used; the weekday roster of this train is on the next page; one may wonder why a diesel fuel depot was not set up at Swanage enabling the train to be stabled there.

Swanage in early BR days. 'M7' class 0-4-4T No. 30111 has the push-pull set in the bay, while through carriages wait in the main platform to be attached to a later train.   *Lens of Sutton*

An evening train at Swanage in June 1964, with Standard 2-6-2T No. 41238, push-pull set No. 616 (not working as such) and an extra Open Third.   *J. Scrace*

'Hampshire' dmu No. 1114 at Swanage on 1st September, 1968; the engine release road had already been lifted.   *D. Gould*

The dmu diagram for 1966

Arrive		Depart	Arrive		Depart
-	Middle Siding No. 1	6.18	17.03½	Swanage	17.32
6.20	Bournemouth	6.30	18.20½	Bournemouth	18.25
7.38½	Weymouth	7.45	19.12½	Swanage	19.48
8.17	Wareham	8.23½	20.08	Wareham	20.43
8.43	Swanage	8.54	21.02½	Swanage	21.15
9.14	Wareham	9.20	22.02	Bournemouth	21.15
9.39½	Swanage	9.48			
10.08	Wareham	10.48		*Wednesdays only*	22.04
11.07½	Swanage	11.45	22.47	Eastleigh	22.50
12.05	Wareham	12.41	23.06	Eastleigh Diesel Depot	
13.00½	Swanage	13.48			
14.08	Wareham	14.41		*Wednesdays excepted*	
15.00½	Swanage	15.10	22.02	Bournemouth	22.30
15.30	Wareham	15.35	22.41	Carriage Sidings WFX	23.30
15.45½	Swanage	16.16	23.40	Middle Siding No. 1	
16.36	Wareham	16.44			

Meanwhile the working of the Bournemouth line had been revolutionised by a system of express push-pull working, using a combination of motored '4-REP' electric sets, 3- and 4-car non-motored sets, and diesel and electro-diesel locomotives. Any combination might be seen; indeed a train with a '4REP' set leading, followed by four or eight unmotored coaches, with a diesel locomotive behind, was quite common. The Swanage branch was catered for by those unmotored '4-TC' sets; in May 1969 for instance a set was attached on weekdays to the 3.30 pm from Waterloo; this reached Swanage at 6.10, had four minutes lay-over, and departed at 6.14 pm for Bournemouth. On Summer Saturdays a set left Waterloo with the 7.57 am, arrived at Swanage at 10.32 am, and left at 10.37 arriving at Waterloo at 1.21 pm attached to a Bournemouth express. The timing of 2 hours 35 minutes compares well with the 3 hours 32 minutes of the 9.18 am through portion of the early 1930s.

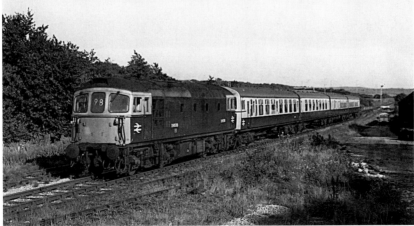

A through train from Swanage to Bournemouth entering Corfe Castle in August 1969. Class '33' No. D6538 is hauling 'TC' set No. 427; these unmotored sets were then working with electric stock to provide through service beyond Bournemouth. *J. Scrace*

A down goods entering Wareham in 1975; the oil depot at that time can be seen behind the signal box.   *Author*

A clay train sets off from Worgret Junction running 'wrong line' in November 1976.   *Author*

The branch was not on the Beeching list of lines destined for the axe, but it seems second thoughts prevailed, for in 1967 it was proposed by British Rail that it should be closed from 9th September, 1968 to passenger service, and should become a freight line serving the clay sidings only. Local opposition to the closure was successful in giving the branch a short further lease of life, but in a climate of widespread closures in other parts of the Region the end could not be long delayed. It was scarcely likely to encourage holiday traffic when the Southern Region's timetables for the period May 1968 to May 1969 proclaimed that the service might be withdrawn during the currency of the timetables! The through carriages ceased; the last runs were, the 7.39 am up from Swanage and 3.30 pm down from Waterloo on 3rd October, 1969. However, local authorities were dissatisfied with the alternative bus services proposed, and succeeded in delaying the final closure until the beginning of 1972; it was in fact on 3rd January of that year that the last state-owned passenger train left Swanage, from a station little more than a ghost, with the engine release road and sidings long gone, the turntable overgrown, and only the fine stone station (mutilated at some stage by the replacement of the LSWR canopy with a convex SR design) to remind one of the great days when only the best was good enough.

However, there were many people who were not prepared to confine their activities to mourning. The preservationists were soon in full cry, with the blessing of Sir John Betjeman, for whom Swanage must surely have represented the epitome of Victorian family holidaymaking which he was recalling so forcefully in print and on television.

The Swanage Railway Society obtained a good press, a little patronising perhaps locally, and they got down to cases. British Rail was asked if it would work trains forward from Worgret; if they would not, then a parallel line from Worgret to Wareham south bay would have to be built. Additional Halts would be put in, at Worgret, Blue Pool, Harman's Cross, and Herston. At least eight trains a day would be run, and a special school train would take 400 children from Swanage to the new 'Comprehensive' at Worgret. A coal terminal would be put in at Swanage, and a terminal for the stone traffic at Harman's Cross.

Resulting from a misunderstanding between the SR estates department and the Swanage Railway Society, contractors began lifting some track in the summer of 1972. Telegrams were sent to various authorities to halt the work, and a petition signed by 2,500 residents was sent to the Minister. A 'Fighting Fund' was also set up. A further misunderstanding caused the destruction of the water tower at Wareham, local officials having concluded that if the Swanage Railway did come about, it would use diesels. By the end of 1972, the railway authorities had informed Dorset County Council and the society that they had only until February to come to a final decision. At the same time, it became known that a property company had made a bid for the site of Swanage station, without which the Swanage Railway could hardly succeed, though contingency plans were made for setting up a terminus beyond Victoria Bridge.

Early in 1973 it was revealed that the local authorities had a plan for building a Corfe by-pass along the route of the railway. The preservationists countered with a suggestion to build a tunnel for the by-pass through the down at the east side of the railway leaving the railway cutting untouched.

Where the lifting stopped; at this point some 300 yards south of the Furzebrook ECC siding, the request to delay lifting the track after closure was heeded; the photograph was taken in October 1976.   *Author*

A clay train pulls out from the Furzebrook works in July 1978, with the oil siding almost completed.   *Author*

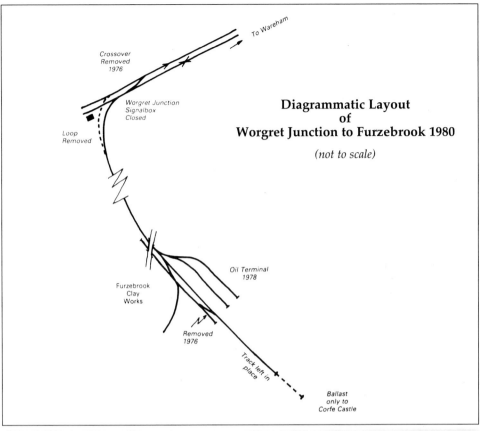

**Diagrammatic Layout
of
Worgret Junction to Furzebrook 1980**

(not to scale)

To Wareham

Crossover
Removed
1976

Worgret Junction
Signalbox
Closed

Loop
Removed

Oil Terminal
1978

Furzebrook
Clay
Works

Removed
1976

Track left in
place

Ballast
only to
Corfe Castle

An oil train at Furzebrook in 1985.   *B.L. Jackson*

A class '47' locomotive heads an oil train near Furzebrook in 1985.   *B.L. Jackson*

Class '60' No. 60 006 *Great Gable* eases out onto the main line at Worgret Junction with a liquid propane gas train on 30th December, 1994.   *Colin Stone*

At the same time work began on restoring the locomotive *Swanage*, a Bulleid Pacific which after withdrawal had been residing in the scrapyards at Barry Docks in South Wales. This engine, No. 34105 in BR days, was not the only one of its class to survive, as another had been at the Liss Steam Centre and was at this time at the Bluebell Railway depot at Sheffield Park, but the fact that the engine was named 'Swanage' provided a rationale for tying it up with the general preservation drive.

However, by the Spring of 1973 the branch track had been lifted, except for the stretch between Worgret Junction and a point 300 yds south of Furzebrook sidings. The English China Clay siding at Furzebrook continued in use, with four or five loaded wagons leaving each day. The Worgret Junction crossover was taken out in November 1976, and thereafter the trains ran 'wrong line' to Wareham, worked by a class '33' diesel. The signal box was removed and the guard of the clay train worked the single point after contacting Wareham signal box.

In November 1977 work began at Furzebrook on a site for a new oil depot on the east side of the clay siding there. An area of several acres was dug out of the heather heath and a siding connection put in from the main line by the bridge. This branched to a short siding and a longer one with loading facilities. Track was in place by June but the first loaded train did not run until 15th December, 1978. The oil came from the Wytch Farm field east of Corfe. Traffic rose to three trains three days per week, which ran to the Hamble refinery on the east side of Southampton Water from August 1985; previously smaller runs had been made to Llandarcy refinery. From January 1986 100 tonne bogie tankers were running to Cadland Wharf, Fawley, on the west side of the Water. Later the oil was pumped by line to the refinery, but the rail link was used for liquid propane gas (to Avonmouth).

Several developments occurred after the line closed. A level crossing was put in just south of Eldon's Siding to give access to the Wytch oilfield. Also the skew bridge over the A351 at Catseye Bridge was rebuilt in steel and widened.

Around 1½ hours late the '6W53', 08.41 Eastleigh to Furzebrook train, hauled by class '66' No. 66 021, approaches Furzebrook with empty LPG tanks on 5th December, 1998.

Colin Stone

The well-known 'Beattie Tank' was the first passenger type on the branch. This example, No. 0298 seen at Exmouth Junction Shed, managed to last into BR ownership as No. 30587 and is now preserved. *Author's Collection*

The '303' class 0-6-0 was used for goods services on the branch up to early SR days; this example, No. 338, was one of the last to go, in 1924. *Lens of Sutton*

Chapter Three

Locomotives and Rolling Stock

It would seem that at first the branch was worked by the well-known 'Beattie Well Tanks', as a photograph exists of No. 209 (of that class) on the train soon after the opening. Even then, however, these engines, which had been built by Beyer, Peacock some 20 years earlier, were thought not to be up to this type of work, and it is probable that they were replaced fairly soon by one of the classes of 4-4-2T. There were three classes of this type, the 'Ironclads' which were rebuilt 4-4-0Ts, the 'steam rollers' with solid bogie wheels, and the class later referred to as the '0522', comprising engines built by a great variety of makers: Beyer, Peacock, Stephensons, Dübs, and Neilson, around 1882-5.

However, although the 'branch engine' itself would have been first a 4-4-2T, then a 'T1' 0-4-4T, later a 'M7' 0-4-4T (from about 1932) and finally a BR 2-6-2T or 2-6-4T, the through trains of all kinds which found their way to Swanage were hauled by a wide range of classes. At first the 'A12' 0-4-2 was a frequent visitor; this class was begun in 1893. The graceful outside cylinder 'X2' and 'T3' 4-4-0s begun a year earlier certainly appeared, and also the similar 'T6' and 'X6' built three years later. After the turn of the century more powerful engines with smaller wheels were preferred: the 'L11' and 'K10' 4-4-0 by Drummond. In the 1930s the 'T9' 4-4-0 sometimes appeared. This numerous class had been started in 1899 for express work, and when Drummond turned his attention to the 4-6-0, these engines descended to lighter work. The smaller 4-4-0s remained more common on the Swanage branch, however, and because of the severe gradients they were very often worked in tandem, or assisted by a tank engine.

Goods traffic was sometimes worked by the '700' class 0-6-0 designed by Drummond and built from 1907 on, though the 'L11' and 'K10' 4-4-0s with only 5 ft 7 in. wheels were equally capable - not that there was much hard work to be done latterly, for the loaded clay wagons would be attached to the train only after most of the climbing had been carried out. No doubt in the early days a fair amount of stone was carried from Swanage, and to lift that up to the 'Corfe Gap' would call for some collar work. In 1938 the new 'Q' class 0-6-0 appeared on the line, but usually in passenger service.

In the early 1960s the 'M7' class began to be joined by Ivatt and BR 2-6-2T and 2-6-4T engines, with occasional visits from BR 2-6-0s, and the branch showed its freedom from cramping restrictions by accepting also the occasional Bulleid 'West Country' Pacific, which of course could not be turned on the Swanage table.

Steam had had a good run, but on 5th September, 1966 the arrival in service of 'Hampshire' 3-coach dmu No. 1104 heralded its end. The last fling was probably the 'Dorset Coast Express', a special which ran down and up the branch on 7th May, 1967 on its way from London to Weymouth, hauled by Bulleid Pacific No. 34023, assisted by 2-6-4T No. 80011. The through trains, now restricted in number, were worked by various classes of diesel locomotive, which also worked the clay traffic, for the short period before passenger closure.

The Adams 'T1' class 0-4-4T was the standard branch engine for 20 years up to the mid-1930s. This example, No. E73, was built in 1889 and not withdrawn until 1936.   *Author*

The 'T6' class was one of several 4-4-0s with 7 ft driving wheels, which worked through trains to Swanage up to the mid-1930s. No. 686 was built in 1896 and is preserved.

Author's Collection

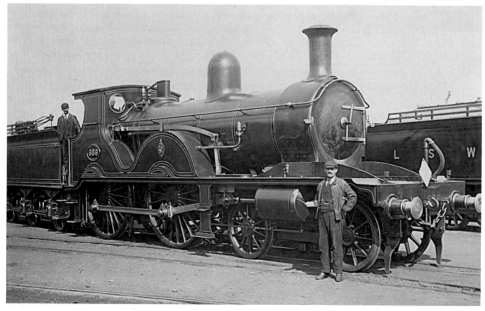

For the first few years of the branch, four-wheeled coaches were used, but by about 1895 bogie coaches would have been appearing on through workings, and soon after 1900 the standard two-coach non-corridor bogie sets would be available, though six-wheeled stock probably also appeared until the 1920s. The 2-8 sets on the branch in the early 1930s normally had a brake compartment at each end, and being fairly short coaches anyway, the seating capacity was small. Whenever there was likely to be extra traffic, loose coaches would be added; by the 1930s these were often corridor coaches. The through workings at that time were a mixture of 2-, 3-, 4-coach corridor sets of the later LSWR or the first Maunsell type. Soon after the SR was formed, Maunsell had ordered some corridor 2-sets in the style of the LSWR 'Ironclads' and these were noted. By 1938 on Saturdays a 7-coach train of later Maunsell stock was rostered to work through to Swanage. After World War II there was less through working, but Bulleid corridor 2-sets appeared occasionally until diesel working began. A number of trains worked through in the summer from the LMS via the Somerset & Dorset, and the author noted in 1932 on a Girl Guide's Special, an LMS low-roofed 12-wheeler - not the kind of thing to be found at the end of many branch lines! With the electrification of lines around Aldershot, more of the ex-LSWR 2-8 push-pull sets became available, and these were often on the branch workings, with suitably-fitted 'M7' 0-4-4Ts, until about 1964, when the 2-6-2Ts which were arriving were not fitted for working them. If as often happened the engine was at the Wareham end, the train after connecting with the through London coaches would comprise the push-pull set leading, then the engine, then the through coaches.

The last batch of 'M7' class engines noted as rostered for Swanage duties, which were alternated with the Brockenhurst branch workings, were Nos. 30031, 30108, 30110, 30112, 30328. The push-and-pull trains which they worked were now made up from Maunsell corridor coaches in the main.

The final type of rolling stock on the branch, apart from the dmu, was the 4-coach unmotored set designed for working in unison with the '4-REP' electric sets which worked from Waterloo to Bournemouth. However, some of the most modern locomotive-hauled stock did make its appearance at Swanage, when the 'Royal Wessex' train from Waterloo to Weymouth was instituted in 1951, with a Swanage portion, as mentioned previously. How sad that a station which could boast of coaches bearing these proud roofboards standing at its platform should so soon have declined to a state that, when one went 'to see the train', there was never anything there but a moaning and juddering dmu, and in only a few years more - no train at all.

A Pullman 'Holiday Coach' (No. P.45 former *Ruby*) was placed at the end of Corfe Castle sidings in the 1960s.

It should be noted that a special goods brake was kept at Wareham for the clay traffic: Maunsell 25 ton No. 55687, lettered 'To work between Wareham and Furzebrook. Not Common User'. This was still in evidence in 1973.

Chapter Four

The Clay Tramways

The kaolonic sedementary clay used for fine ceramics is rare and occurs in a few patches in the South of England and West Country, in deposits from 30 to 50 feet in depth. In Purbeck, geological folding has brought parts of the Creekmoor Deposit to the surface, and the clay has been worked from the Iron Age and in Roman times.

By 1669 it is on record as for sale at 5s. 4d. per ton 'delivered to Russell Point at Arne'. Extraction continued during the 18th century, mainly for clay pipe production, but soon demand from the porcelain manufacturers in Staffordshire rose to the point where a number of merchants became interested, and the titled landowners of Purbeck were pressured to grant leases of lands in the clay areas, almost all heathland.

The Pike Brothers of Wareham, and a Londoner, Benjamin Fayle, were prominent; the former lived locally at Furzebrook House, but the Fayle family remained in London and employed a manager.

Fayle, a shipping agent by trade, bought some clay pits at Norden off a Mr Chiffney around 1800, moving it by pack horse across two miles of heath to Poole Harbour at Middlebere. However in 1806 he replaced them by a well engineered tramroad and no doubt improved the quay. The Pikes continued to use pack horses to their wharf at Wareham until 1838, when they purchased land for a quay at Ridge from Lord Rivers, and laid a railway across Stoborough Heath.

In the 1840s the Staffordshire potters formed a 'Clay Company' to distribute material evenly amongst companies. It would appear also that at this time a firm in Newton Abbot was marketing clay from Furzebrook, presumably along with South Devon clay.

The clay was normally sold in oblong chunks called 'balls' (some say because a Turbal spade was used in digging it). The method of working open-cast sites did not change for a century. After overburden, mostly peat, was taken off, the clay 'floor' was cut into vertical sections with a specific spade, leaving another 'floor' when cleared. The end sections on each floor were left in place, so that as work went down, the cutting would have stepped sides. The balls were moved on light rails to the edge of the pit where they were reloaded into larger wagons for movement to beds, where they would weather for a month or more to wash out impurities.

Most pits were long cuttings, but some round pits were dug, and there were also adits and shafts where the clay was some way below the surface.

The Middlebere Plateway

This was built by Benjamin Fayle from his pits at Norden near Corfe Castle, to a wharf on Middlebere Creek, a channel running south from the Wytch Channel at Poole Harbour. In its first year it would have terminated at some small pits on the east side of the Wareham road. The plateway pursued a winding course to provide a level enough track for horse-haulage, though some shallow cutting was required in the middle part of Middlebere Heath, and tunnels under the Wareham Road as described later.

Although plateways and railways were becoming known in the North, they were rare in the South; when the Swanage peninsular was mapped in 1811 by Lt-Col Madge, the only sign of industrial activity he noted was the 'Iron Rail Way' to Middlebere; he spotted two passing loops, and it would be interesting to know the thoughts of an old soldier of that time about this new-fangled thing.

The Middlebere line is first described in *A General View of the Agriculture of Dorset* by William Stevenson, published in 1812. He states that it was built in 1806 and was 3½ miles long; the tramplates were three feet long, the vertical and horizontal sides both measuring three inches. The stone sleepers weighed 60-70 lb. each (they had two circular depressions into which bosses on the inside ends of the plates fitted to make them more stable). The plates were fastened with one spike in an oak plug. The gradient is given as 1 in 150 to 1 in 180, and the whole work cost £2,000 per mile. The wagons carried two tons of clay each and three horses drew five wagons at a cost of 6d. per ton.

An isolated mention in Farey's *General View of Agriculture in Derbyshire* (1817) notes that 'Collinge's patent axletree has been applied to the trams on the Rail-ways to the famous pipe-clay pits near Corfe Castle'. This axle, patented in 1811, was largely used for road vehicles and no other application to railway vehicles is known. It implies that the wheels revolved on fixed axles, which was commonly the case with plateway vehicles, some examples of which from other plateways have been preserved.

Stevenson stated that the clay was being shipped from Middlebere in sea-going craft to places such as Liverpool. However, Fayle only claimed that the clay was shipped 'almost direct' to the Mersey, so it was probably barged to Poole for re-loading from the first.

Shortly after opening it was necessary to tunnel under the road. There are in fact two tunnels; the northern one has a plaque on the east face reading 'BF 1807'; the southern one has on its west face 'Dated in 1848'. As this tunnel appears on earlier tithe maps this must be a rebuilding date. Both tunnels are very low, and the horses had to have special harnesses which did not project upwards at all. The remains of both tracks now pass through one skew tunnel under the LSWR, but as the southern track has a very serpentine course it probably originally made junction the other side of the LSWR near the smithy and washing beds at New Line Farm, but was slewed to allow the LSWR to build only one tunnel under itself.

At the Middlebere end there was a siding and turntable on the wharf, and a siding to a slipway. There was also a flagpole; this could have been to signal to a ship in the main channel to come in, or it could have been to let someone inland know that a ship was putting in.

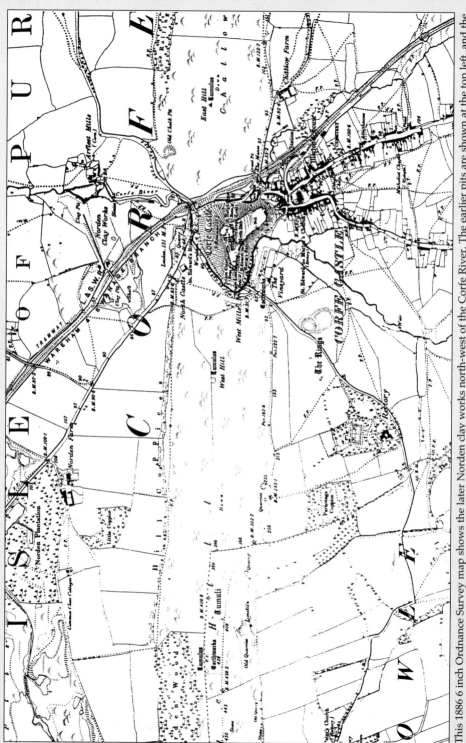

This 1886 6 inch Ordnance Survey map shows the later Norden clay works north-west of the Corfe River. The earlier pits are shown at the top left, and the connection between the two is marked 'tramway'.

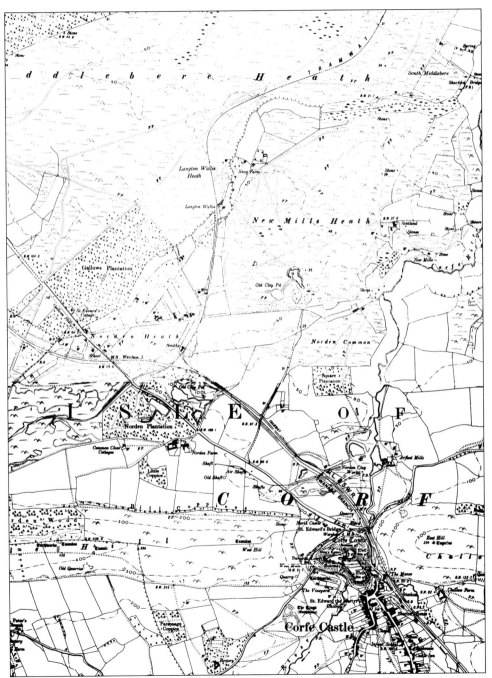

A map of the Corfe area (*c.* 1890) showing the course of the Middlebere Plateway.

The west face of the north tunnel, note the keystone reading 'BF 1807'; taken in 1975.   *Author*

The east face of the south tunnel at Norden, showing the plaque reading 'Dated in 1848' and thought to have been rebuilt at that time.   *Author*

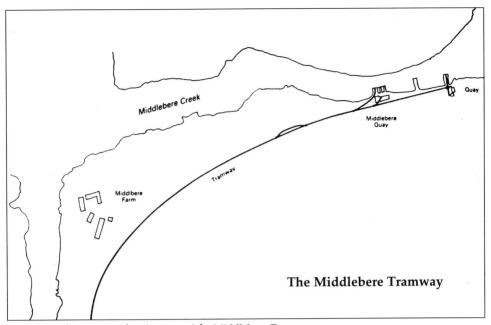

The Middlebere Tramway

The northern end of the plateway of the Middlebere Tramway.

The first passing loop on the Middlebere tramroad, from the south, as it was in April 1938.

Author

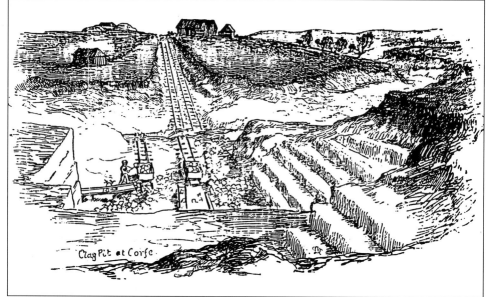

An illustration from Robinson's *Picturesque Rambles in the Isle of Purbeck* (1882). This Fayle's pit is believed to have been between the later LSWR cutting at Norden and the main road.

A stone sleeper in place on the Middlebere tramroad in May 1972; note the two round indentations on the left of the spike hole, in which protrusions at the ends of the plates were located.   *Author*

Benjamin Fayle first introduced himself to the potters by letter on 26th July, 1804 while on a visit to Newcastle (Staffs), stating that he had appointed Mr John Scarlet of Newcastle as agent for blue and brown clays from the estates of William Morton Pitt and John Calcraft. He wrote on 16th August, 1806 saying he had completed his 'Iron rail-way' and offering clay on board ships at 18s. per ton. By 1813 he was writing from Hanley hoping that Wedgwood would visit Norden. It is clear from the letter that he was in strong competition with other suppliers, probably in Devon.

In 1882 a Mr Robinson published *Picturesque Rambles in the Isle of Purbeck* in which a claypit is illustrated being dug 'on the east side of the Corfe road' which would seem to be where the iron bridge over the LSWR was later located. He refers to the clay being transported to Goathorn (an error for Middlebere) 'by a tramway having a flange to retain wheels of trucks'. This suggests that a branch from the tramway at the smithy must have been laid southwards past the later site of Eldon Siding. This was later edge-rail and is dealt with in the section on Fayle's Tramway.

The curious appearance of the iron bridge, which is still in place, suggests that originally it sloped from east to west into a pit, but had to be built up at the west side when the track was continued across the main road.

The Newton Tramway

Newton, on the southern edge of Poole Harbour, is a modern 'lost village'. Before World War II there was a community here, with men working at the clay pits which had been started by Fayle's some time around 1860. Two pits were dug to the south of the village which ultimately reached some half-mile in length. The clay was transported on a tramway to a pier on the Goathorn peninsular, nearly two miles away, which lay on a waterway known as the South Deep. Its early form is not known; it is rumoured that it was of 3 ft 6 in. gauge and horse-worked, but Fayle's acquired the Stephen Lewin engine (see Fayle's Tramway section) of 3 ft 9 in. gauge and it may have worked here.

The layout as it consisted in the 1930s comprised a depot close to the convergence of the two long pits, with various buildings including a possible engine shed, and a much older building possibly a stable, and the two mile 3 ft 9 in. gauge tramway to Goathorn depot. Here there was a three-line stub-point layout, the right-hand one going into a large store with living attachment, and the other two forming a loop. At the end of the loop was a further 50 yards of track, opening up to a further loop on a wooden staging with a metal shute at the end worked by a hand winch.

From about 1905 the layout was linked to Fayle's Norden works, and this line is covered in the Fayle's Tramway section. During World War II the village was destroyed in army exercises and nothing remained but a few piles of bricks. Goathorn Pier was dismantled and the shute and winch thrown into the water. The pit area was taken over by the Forestry and became overgrown. There is much still to learn about activities at Newton.

A picturesque view of the Newton Tramway in Goathorn Plantation in April 1938.   *Author*

Goathorn depot in 1938; the left hand rail leading into the shed has been laid over the other, and provided with wood blocks to cross over the loop rail; only a light wagon was in use. Track to the pier shute in the distance was not in use at the time.   *Author*

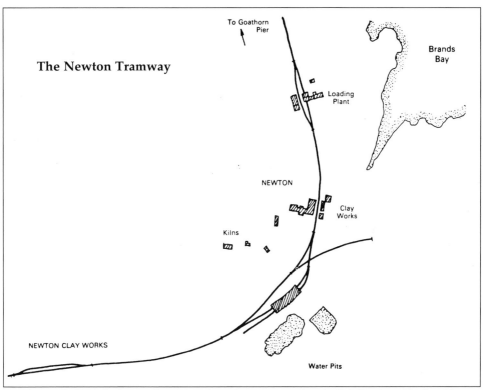

Newton in 1886; the loop at the west end was later connected to the link line from Norden. The long claypits running south-west for half a mile off the bottom of the plan are not marked here.

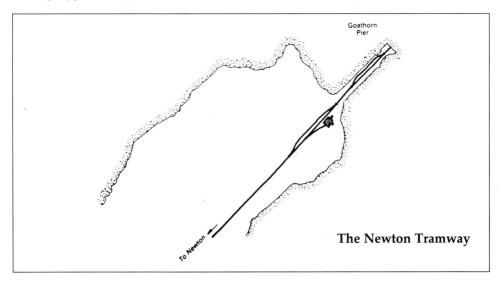

The end of the easternmost Newton pit on Newton Heath in 1977, approximately half a mile from the depot. The neat stepped-sided pits were soon weathered into untidy depressions. *Author*

A wagon and winch thrown off the pier at Goathorn during World War II; seen here in 1977. *Author*

Fayle's Tramway

This is the title normally given to the 5¾ mile system after the connection to Newton had been made. The date of abandonment of the Middlebere Plateway is not certain, but probably about 1907 (incorrectly given in B. Baxter's book as 1866). The south-east extension from the smithy mentioned above was quite possibly plateway, and the later extension across the road to Norden Farm may have been, also a branch running north-east to an incline which served low lying pits west of the Corfe River. However, the link line to Newton was a normal railway, and it seems likely that edge-rail was laid past Eldon Siding to the smithy before the turn of the century.

At about the time that the Middlebere Tramroad fell out of use, rails were laid from a point just south-east of the Slepe Road bridge across the heath to join the Newton Tramway. There was a locomotive shed east of the junction, where the track turned north-east and then east, with a short branch at Bushey running south, and a loop just before the track ran into Newton depot. It was mostly level through sand and peat, but with one light wooden overbridge on stone piers, for a dirt track. Flat-bottom rail was spiked to wooden sleepers with earth ballast. Pointwork was normal and not of the stub type found elsewhere on Fayle's.

The layout at Norden was constantly changing, with wooden buildings being put up or moved; after World War II a large building was put up where the Newton line had diverged, to process clay. Basically in the 1930 to 1970 period there was a large depot with mines and pits west of the main road; the line crossed the road (guarded by a stub-catchpoint) passing some sidings to cross the Swanage branch to a dead-end which had once been the head of an incline down to lower pits. Trains reversed out of here and ran down via weathering beds alongside the SR branch to a long loop having a weighbridge on its north track, and on to pass under Slepe Road to the loading platform of Eldon's Siding (renamed Norden Siding by British Rail). The track to the locomotive shed and Newton ran down from the north end of the weighbridge loop.

Because of the reversal at the incline all loaded trains had the engine in front crossing the main road, and at the rear going to Eldon's Siding. At the siding there was a short spare track between the two tracks of the loop, and a wagon shelter over part of the northern track. An all-over shelter was added about 1950. Eldon's Siding was not used in the late 1960s, and clay was loaded into lorries at a temporary shute located at a track underpass near the present Norden station.

Fayle's Tramway was using normal railway track, to a gauge of 3 ft 9 in., and had two steam locomotives. One was a very small 0-4-0T built by Stephen Lewin of Poole about 1875, said to have originally been *Corfe* and later *Tiny*, though it bore no name by 1930. The other was a larger Manning, Wardle 0-4-0ST (Works No. 1552 built 1902) purchased in 1909 from the Northern Outfall sewerage line of the LCC at Barking, and converted from 3 ft 6 in. gauge. This must have been purchased for the long haul to Goathorn, as it was too high to pass under the road bridge between Norden depot and the exchange sidings. (In 1938 the track was lowered under the bridge to enable it to do so.) This engine retained its name *Thames* on cast plates on the saddle tanks and number 48 on cab-side. This was the engine used to run the line's 'passenger service'

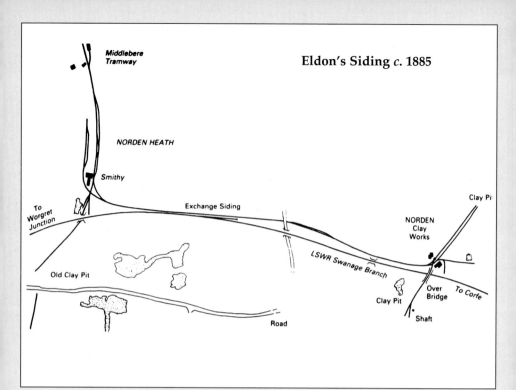

Eldon's Siding *c.* 1885

Middlebere Tramway

NORDEN HEATH

Smithy

To Worgret Junction

Exchange Siding

Old Clay Pit

Road

NORDEN Clay Works

Clay Pit

LSWR Swanage Branch

Clay Pit

Over Bridge

To Corfe

Shaft

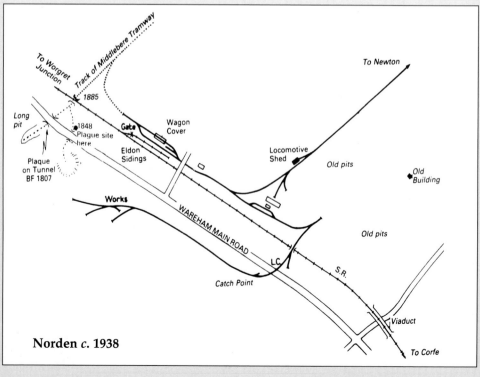

Norden *c.* 1938

To Worgret Junction

Track of Middlebere Tramway

1885

To Newton

Long pit

1848
Plaque site here

Plaque on Tunnel BF 1807

Gate

Eldon Sidings

Wagon Cover

Locomotive Shed

Old pits

Old Building

Works

WAREHAM MAIN ROAD

Old pits

LC

S.R.

Catch Point

Viaduct

To Corfe

As the Lewin engine propels a loaded train to Eldon's Siding in August 1932, the Manning, Wardle which had drawn clear of the points with empties, comes forward to take them across the road to the west pit. *Author*

From the footplate of the Lewin engine at Eldon's Siding on 23rd August, 1932. The engine will draw out the empties, run them through the shelter, and return with more loaded wagons waiting in the middle siding. The signal visible to the left of the chimney is the down distant for Corfe at Slepe Lane bridge. *Author*

The simple construction of the wagons is clear, as the Lewin engine pulls four empties out on the line to the former smithy, before reversing round loaded wagons at Eldon Siding in 1932.
Author

The Manning, Wardle engine, *Thames*, at Norden in 1932; it is still carrying its LCC number, 48, on the cab side.   *Author*

from 1920 to 1936 after Newton school was converted to a chapel. *Thames* and a converted clay wagon with a corrugated-iron roof conveyed schoolchildren daily from Newton to Corfe for a return fare of 7s. 6d. (somewhat high for some six miles; possibly the contemporary report was in error and it was 7s. 6d. per week). An extra shed was built opposite the locomotive shed where the Newton link line met the Norden workings, to accommodate the 'coach'.

There is no photograph of the Manning, Wardle engine in its early days; as seen in the 1930s it had a modified cab, suggesting an attempt may have been made to fit it through the Arne Road bridge, but even so it could not go through until the track was later lowered, and it may have been done by its original owner.

Some light 22 in. gauge track was used at Norden between shafts and weathering beds. Small wooden wagons, some with eyed straps for vertical lifting were in use.

The engine *Tiny* will be described in some detail, since like all Lewin engines she seems to have been unique, whereas *Thames* was of course a standard design. Her principal dimensions were: cylinders 5 in. x 9 in., boiler pressure 120 lb. (later 160 lb.); wheels 1 ft 9 in. diameter (later 1 ft 7 in.), wheelbase 3 ft 10 in., boiler diameter 2 ft 4 in; tank capacity 130 gallons, coal 4 cwt., weight in working order 7 tons. She was certainly rebuilt at various times, she had new cylinders in 1916, these being stamped 'Dorset Iron Foundry', a firm with some connections with Lewin. At the time the author knew her best (about 1930) she had a stove-pipe chimney, large brass dome on the first boiler ring and polished bands around the cylinders. This engine had the top of its cab backplate, with two square windows, able to hinge down, presumably to pass through the narrow bridge over the line just short of Eldon Siding. The buffers were wood-faced, and the brake blocks were of wood and a cylinder lubricator was mounted in front of the chimney.

In 1938 *Tiny* got her last new boiler, from Bagnalls, and this was the one which later was mounted on one of the Pikes' engines; about the same time she was fitted with a proper cab, a luxury which was customarily omitted at the time she was built, but which in less kind climates than that of Dorset became *de rigeur* much earlier.

Several building dates for *Tiny* have been suggested; one was 1868, because there was a rumour that someone had found some spare cylinders in the shed bearing this date, but the authors of the definitive history of Stephen Lewin discount this, saying the cylinders were probably from some other equipment. The dates 1870 and 1873 have also been given (the latter to the author by her driver). Nor is it clear what she did on arrival; Mr C.N. Sykes says that she worked on the Middlebere line but was withdrawn as 'she cracked the rails' - this would apply to tram-plates, in which case unflanged wheels would have been provided. Maybe she worked at Newton, opened in 1868, and she really was built in that year: the debate continues.

The wagons were short unsprung four-wheelers with three outside frame members supporting the low planked sides. The dumb buffers were set at the extreme edges of the buffer beam, forming in fact an extension of the frame to which the axle boxes were bolted. One end of the body could be dropped over the buffers for loading.

The Lewin engine crosses the iron bridge with a load from the pits in August 1938; two wagons of loose material, and two piled high with 'balls'. *Author*

The Lewin engine at Norden in 1932. Unconfirmed dimensions are: wheels 1 ft 7 in., wheelbase
3 ft 10 in., cylinders 5 in. x 9 in. A screw brake was on the far side.   *Author*

The Lewin engine from the rear, in 1932, showing the top of the cab back-plate folded down to
improve clearance. The 'spectacles' were blanked in this position.   *Author*

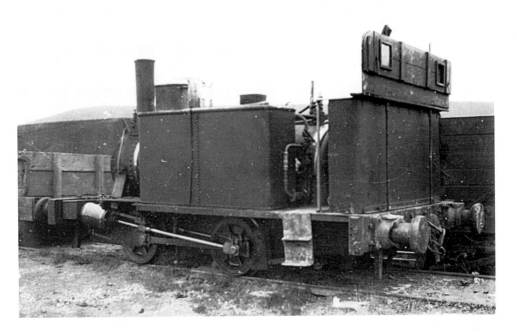

Though generally a surface line, the link track passed under a light bridge in a short cutting east of Bushey. Taken in 1932.   *Author*

Russell on Fayle's Tramway after the leading axle had been removed, and on the day in August 1953 when a further boiler certificate had been refused.   *J.I.C. Boyd*

It is not certain that any were former plateway wagons, though their low build suggests a design suited to the early tunnels. The fact that some were numbered in the 90s must mean that a lot of early wagons had been scrapped. (The high numbers on the later 2 ft wagons were probably applied before they were acquired.)

Roads suitable for motor traffic were now penetrating the heathland, and the role of Fayle's Tramway as the only way from Corfe to Poole Harbour was passing. It is of interest that in the late 1920s stone was taken down the tramway to Goathorn for shipping and dumping at the 'training bank' which protects the entrance to Poole Harbour between Studland and Sandbanks.

By 1937 the Newton line seemed to be little used. On a visit at Easter of that year, *Tiny* was doing its usual chores between the Norden pits and Eldon Siding and *Thames* was in the newly-erected ancillary locomotive shed, together with the 'coach'. From here to Newton the rails showed no sign of recent use, but the portion between Goathorn Pier and Newton village was being 'operated' by a trolley carrying a large barrel bearing the word 'Oporto'. One presumes that it carried water rather than port, and that the water was travelling from the village to the pier.

During World War II much of the line across Newton Heath was taken up and there was no working north of the engine shed. When therefore in 1948 it was decided to re-gauge the line to 1 ft 11½ in., there was not a great mileage to be dealt with. To work the narrow gauge line, one steam engine and several internal combustion-engined rail tractors were purchased. The steam engine was *Russell*, a 2-6-2T by Hunslet (1906) with a chequered history. She had been built for the Portmadoc, Beddgelert & South Snowdon Railway, which never got as far as opening, and she went to work for the associated North Wales Narrow Gauge Railway. When this railway became part of the Welsh Highland Railway, she was rather severely butchered to reduce her vertical clearance enough to go through the notorious Moelwyn tunnel on the Festiniog Railway, it being intended to haul through trains from Dinas Junction to Festiniog. She got through the tunnel - only just, once - but continued mainly working the Beddgelert-Dinas section, until 1936 when the line closed. A spell of five years in Dinas shed was followed by six years working for the Ministry of Supply at the Hook Norton mines in Oxfordshire, and in 1948 *Russell* came south to Norden. But there was not much life left in her. The leading axle gave trouble and she latterly worked as a 0-6-2T. In 1953 a further boiler certificate was refused, and she was purchased by the Birmingham Locomotive Club for exhibition at the Narrow Gauge Museum at Towyn in North Wales, being moved in August 1955. Ten years of standing in the open by the road bridge over Towyn Wharf station did little to improve her, and when on 15th April, 1965 she was moved yet again, to the protection of the Welsh Highland Railway Society, there was much work to be done on her if she were to steam again. (This work has now been finished and *Russell* works at Portmadoc.) Latterly there were five internal combustion engines, built by Orenstein & Koppel, Motor Rail and Lister.

On the new gauge, the clay wagons were steel tippers, though one or two of the old wagons were re-gauged for special purposes. However, the use of stub-points continued and Fayle's Tramway remained an interesting oddity

The ex-Welsh Highland Railway 2-6-2T *Russell* hauling empty wagons away from Eldon's Siding in August 1949, on the newly-laid 2 ft gauge track. The new processing sheds can just be seen behind the weighbridge on the right.   *Author*

Russell out of use in 1955 in the siding between the bridge and road at Norden. The Orenstein & Koppel diesel is passing with a loaded train from the pits.   *J.R. Bonser*

performing a very useful job. In 1949 Fayle's had amalgamated with its neighbour, Pike's, and when in 1956 the latter turned over to road transport it seemed likely that Fayle's would do the same in due course. One reason was that customers were now accepting clay in bulk rather than in 'balls' and unweathered, so that the complex rail-served weathering beds were not needed.

After World War II there was little left around Newton; at Goathorn the winchgear had been thrown into the water along with a wagon, and the pier demolished. Only rubble remained around the village; a few small kilns were left, some using pieces of light flat-bottomed rail suggesting the tramway there must originally have been horse-worked. By 1969 Eldon's Siding was overgrown and point-clamped; in October of that year a driver stated that the last train would cross the bridge within weeks, but in fact some working continued. In April 1970 an enthusiast noted a full train in a siding west of the main road, and two engines and 18 wagons standing on the east side lines. One year later after track-lifting had begun, an engine was working with flat wagons on the west side. All track was lifted on the east side apart from that in the old engine shed, but on the other side some 2 ft track was left; also much 22 in. track was *in situ* with tubs on it, and a cableworked adit at the north end was still working in 1978.

Most of the equipment moved piecemeal to scrap, but one of the Orenstein & Koppel diesels was sold to a lady in Hampshire who had a railway; the other was not in usable condition.

The engine shed at Norden in 1955, with the front wheels removed from *Russell* lying by the track. The small shed at the left had been used for the school 'carriage' pre-war.

J.R. Bonser

The east sidings at Norden in 1969. The siding into the large shed was a late addition; to the right of it can be seen the weighbridge and loop, with the line to the engine shed passing to its left.

Author

This 'broad gauge' wagon has been cut down and regauged for the 2 ft system; a diesel tank wagon at Norden in 1969.   *Author*

Above left: The catch point at Norden protecting the Corfe road comprised a 'blade' attached by old rail to a lever, which could slide over the first four sleepers with balks on the first two to prevent spreading.   *Author*

Above right: The locomotive shed in 1969 was far from what action remained, and little used. This was the only stub point on the relaid system.   *Author*

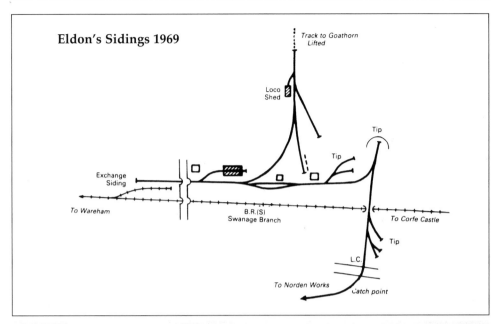

Eldon's Sidings 1969

Track to Goathorn Lifted

Loco Shed

Tip

Exchange Siding

To Wareham

B.R.(S) Swanage Branch

To Corfe Castle

Tip

L.C.

To Norden Works

Catch point

Eldon's Siding in 1972, showing the pointwork and the ground frame on the up side of the main line, opposite the gate. *Author*

The dead-end at which all trains from across the iron bridge had to reverse to run to Eldon's Siding; photographed in October 1969.   *Author*

The Lister engine in the weighbridge loop in 1969.   *Author*

Bogie flat wagons in 1969 at the site of the processing sheds which had been demolished. They had centre couplers and hand brake on one bogie.   *Author*

A covered shaft at the western Norden workings in 1975, showing the narrow gauge wagons used internally.   *Author*

The adit at the end of the Norden complex in June 1978; the cable haulage was electric-powered.
Author

The smallest wagons used at Norden were fitted with lifting eyes; this one was left on the surface after the clearance, in 1978.   *D. Gould*

Pike Brothers' Tramway

W.J. and J.W. Pike were operating as clay merchants, from about 1760, when they purchased Furzebrook House, south of Wareham, and were selling to Wedgwood by 1791. The clay came from a large pit a few hundred yards south of the House. For some reason, perhaps land ownership, they were unable to follow Fayle's lead until 1830, when a railway said to have been of 4 ft gauge was laid with ruler straightness to the hamlet of Ridge, on the Wareham Channel, ending beside a short canal, though later extended to the river front.

It was downhill all the way, and worked by gravity and horses until 1866, when it was relaid in 'T' section rail heavy enough to take locomotives.

Working was now around Creech and the line by-passed Furzebrook House to a well equipped depot at the top end of the long straight. In addition a locomotive shed was erected in Ridge; Pikes owned a slipway and the engine was used among other things to haul boats up the slipway. There were two loops, the longer one serving washing beds north of Ridge itself.

Various mines were opened to the west, at Povington, Cotness, Greenspecks and Creech Grange; though the track on the 'main line' was of 2 ft 8½ in. gauge, in the mines 22 inch track was used. At Cotness, which was a very large mine, the narrow rails ran on to a large wooden platform above the wider track.

A siding on the Swanage branch was put in at some time after 1900, comprising a track on a grade of 1 in 300 towards Worgret, with a spur into the tranship bay, where the narrow gauge metals were high enough to permit tipping into the rail wagons. A point at the south end of the siding allowed an engine to run round, necessary when the siding became the end of the line, but probably not when the trip goods was working and could insert or take out wagons on its up journey. The clay company had no standard gauge engine and any shunting would have been done by the LSWR, and later by SR and BR. The bridge over the Stoborough Heath road adjacent to the siding was built for double track and in fact the siding track was laid through it.

The so-called 'blue pool' at Furzebrook is said to have been the first working by the Pike brothers. *Photo Precision*

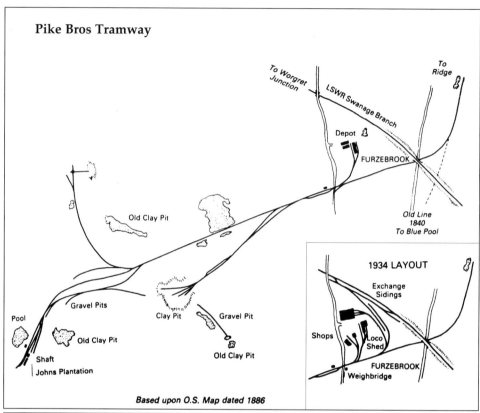

Pike Bros Tramway

To Worgret Junction

LSWR Swanage Branch

To Ridge

Depot

FURZEBROOK

Old Clay Pit

Old Line 1840 To Blue Pool

Gravel Pits

Pool

Clay Pit

Gravel Pit

Old Clay Pit

Old Clay Pit

Shaft

Johns Plantation

Based upon O.S. Map dated 1886

1934 LAYOUT

Exchange Sidings

Shops

Loco Shed

FURZEBROOK

Weighbridge

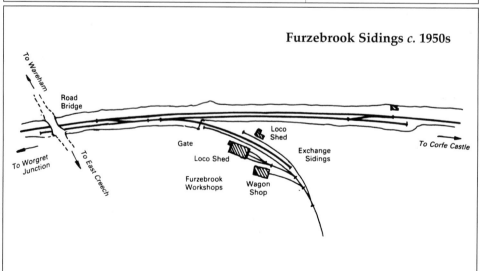

Furzebrook Sidings *c.* **1950s**

To Wareham

Road Bridge

To Worgret Junction

To East Creech

Gate

Loco Shed

Loco Shed

Furzebrook Workshops

Wagon Shop

Exchange Sidings

To Corfe Castle

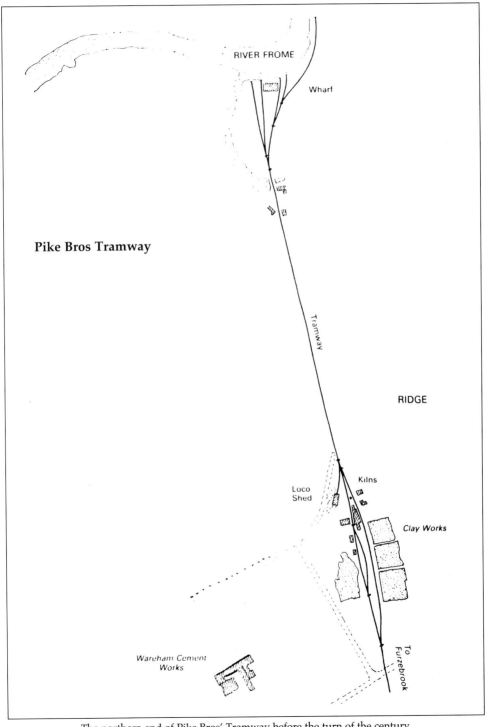

RIVER FROME

Wharf

Pike Bros Tramway

Tramway

RIDGE

Kilns

Loco
Shed

Clay Works

Wareham Cement
Works

To
Furzebrook

The northern end of Pike Bros' Tramway before the turn of the century.

Pike Brothers' *Secundus* on the main line; ahead the track passes under the SR, and to the left it curves round to the works. Taken in 1938.

Author

At Ridge, just short of the wharf, was another small works and a locomotive shed (still standing). A long loop ran round the works here, with a smaller loop in the 'main line' adjacent to the depot.

No doubt gravity-working was still sometimes employed; even in the 1930s the workers who lived at Ridge returned home by gravity sitting in a single braked wagon. Some of the wagons had sledge brakes (i.e. acting on the rail itself) and such powerful braking suggests gravity runs. The line to Ridge crossed the Wareham road on the level; this crossing was protected by a catch-point on the Furzebrook side and by a heavy hinged beam across the track on the other side. When the workers came down in their wagon, one would jump off, hold the catch-point lever over, double across the road to lift the beam, then jump back on the wagon without it coming to a stand - this sort of dexterity was found on many mineral railways up and down the country.

The locomotive history is not entirely clear, as the company kept no records, but the following list is as comprehensive as records allow:

Primus: a six-wheeler, probably 0-4-2WT, bought from a firm called Bellis & Seekings in 1866, and scrapped some 30 years later.

Secundus: an 0-6-0T of odd design, also bought from Bellis & Seekings in 1874, with enclosed motion and 'cow-catchers' which suggest it may have been designed as a street tramway engine. It also had a marine type boiler. This engine is now preserved.

Tertius: an 0-6-0ST by Manning, Wardle built in 1886 (No. 999); of their standard design, but made very non-standard at the end of its career when in 1951 the boiler of the Lewin engine from Norden was fitted to it which, having a firebox too wide to pass within the frames, was perched above them!

Quartus: said to be an 0-4-2WT by Fowler, purchased in 1889, scrapped 1934.

Quintus: a Manning, Wardle 0-4-0ST (No. 1854 of 1914), which worked until 1956.

Sextus: a Peckett 0-4-2ST of 1925 (No. 1692), which also worked until 1956.

Septimus: a Peckett 0-4-2ST of 1930 (No. 1808) which differed from the above in being somewhat smaller. This engine was purchased in 1955 by the North Somerset Light Railway, which was to have run from Worle to Clevedon over the bed of the old Weston Clevedon & Portishead Railway, but which never opened. It went to Peckett's works in 1956 and was scrapped by Joseph Pugsley of Bristol early in 1962.

The main dimensions were:

	length over buffers	*total wheelbase*	*coupled wheels*
Secundus	11 ft 10 in.	6 ft 0 in.	2 ft 8 in.
Tertius	15 ft 0 in.	7 ft 6 in.	2 ft 0 in.
Quintus	16 ft 9 in.	4 ft 6 in.	2 ft 0 in.
Sextus	18 ft 10 in.	10 ft 0 in.	2 ft 6½ in.
Septimus	17 ft 8 in.	9 ft 6 in.	2 ft 3 in.

In 1951 a Simplex diesel locomotive was bought, second-hand. The diesel-oil tank which was set up on a stage at Furzebrook for fuel later saw service mounted on a converted 'broad gauge' wagon on the Norden line.

In 1955 road transport began taking over, the first section to go (early in the year) being Cotness. Greenspecks followed in the summer, and the last run to Creech Grange was on 30th July, 1956. The weathering beds were rail-worked for a further year. The Povington mine was on Army land and may have been disused before the rest of the branch.

Pike's *Tertius* near Furzebrook in July 1955; the third wagon has the sledge brake, the other two simple brakes. The train is propelling to the works, visible behind the tree.   *J.R. Bonser*

Tertius was given the fairly new boiler off Fayle's Lewin engine in 1951, but its firebox was too wide to fit between the frames, and had to be placed above them.   *J.R. Bonser*

Pike Brothers' *Sextus* receiving attention to its slide bars outside the Furzebrook engine shed in August 1932.   *Author*

The 0-4-2ST *Septimus* outside the engine shed at Furzebrook in August 1938; on the left is the wagon repair shed.   *Author*

Workers from Furzebrook riding back to Ridge by gravity in August 1932. The member of the party who has held the catch point the other side of the road, and lifts the stop block this side, will jump aboard.   *Author*

The riding wagon No. 48 in a short siding at Ridge. Sprung buffer beams were only fitted at one end.   *Author*

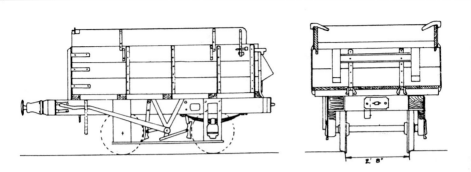

Furzebrook Tramway (Pike Bros, Fayle & Co. Ltd) 4-ton end door wagon (in original condition).
Built by Cambrian Wagon Co.
Drawn from information by Cambrian Wagon Co. and photographic evidence.

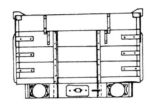

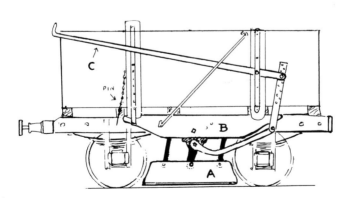

Pike's Tramway: operating method of sledge brake; pushing down the lever C causes sledge A
to bear on the running rail, acting against thrust beam B fixed to side of wagon.

Ridge engine shed and drying sheds in August 1932. The engine shed, believed built in 1866, was 'listed' in 1998.

Author

In the early days 'T-bulb' rail in chairs was used: some remain as fenceposts today. Later flat-bottom track was used, and in the mines themselves some 22 in. gauge light bridge rail has been found.

The wagon stock comprised end-tipping, side-tipping, and fixed wagons of various kinds, some built by the Cambrian Wagon Co. and some locally. One of the sledge-braked wagons was rescued and sent to the Towyn Narrow Gauge Museum. Buffer beams were sprung at one end only, by a leaf-spring set transversely between beam and frame. This did not apply to the end-tippers which were mostly used in the mine areas; these had only dumb buffers.

Although the wagons appeared to be of great antiquity, one enthusiast who came to mourn at the pyre of burning wagon stock in November 1957 reported that some had maker's plates as late as 1936.

One curious feature of the end-tippers was that the body overhung the frame at one end, with a space at the other end; thus if all were lined up with the tipping end facing the weathering beds, all was fine; but the engines had to work with flat-wagons attached so as to be able to couple to a tipping end if required.

Some of the 1 ft 10 in. gauge tramways in the clay workings continued in use after the Furzebrook Tramway itself closed: in 1968 the Pikes' undertaking was purchased by English China Clays.

Secundus is preserved in the Newhall Street Museum in Birmingham: a very interesting though hardly typical specimen of Victorian engineering. How many of her oddities, which include outside Stephenson's valve gear, were due to a rebuilding by Stephen Lewin in 1880 is hard to say.

There have been some investigations of Middlebere. In 1961 J.K.W. Davies recovered a plateway frog and in 1964 a plate dug up by M. Lewis was sent to Ironbridge Museum. L. Popplewell reported that a turntable had been dug up and re-buried. More recently M. Wilmott has dug in two places and found that near the wharf there are sleepers at spacings of 5 to 6 feet, instead of the normal 3 feet, possibly for some installation, perhaps a 'balling' machine for balls broken on the tramroad. He found the distance between peg-holes in sleepers to be 46 in. suggesting a gauge of 3 ft 6 in. rather than the 3 ft 9 in. often quoted.

The rails across the main road north of Furzebrook remained through several resurfacings and were finally lifted in 1981.

A section of the rail laid in 1866 for steam working on Pikes' Tramway; used as a fence post and photographed in 1975. *Author*

This print by R. Sydenham of Poole showing a long run of stone wagons approaching Swanage old pier seems to be dated 1856 though opening is usually given as 1858.

An old photograph of the original two-line terminus of the Swanage Pier Tramway at the stone 'bankers'. This gives a good idea of the volume of the stone traffic, and was probably taken in about 1880. This part has long been built over.   *Swanage Library*

Chapter Five

Other Tramways

The Swanage Pier Tramway

This line was one-third of a mile long, and ran from the old pier to stone stores and a coal depot along the seafront. The Tramway was designed by Capt. W. Moorsom, Chief Engineer of the Southampton & Dorchester Railway, and seems to have been opened in 1858, notwithstanding a print of it published in Poole dated August 1856. The gauge was latterly 2 ft 6 in. but wider originally. The pier was built to obviate the rather dangerous practice of horse-carts going out into the waters of the bay to load stone onto barges. There was a plan to build a tramway from the pier to the stone quarries at Langton Matravers. There can be little doubt that at any rate until the coming of the LSWR there was considerable traffic in stone up the pier line, but it does not seem that mechanical traction was used. At the time the author first knew it (in the 1930s) only one wagon remained, apparently used for carrying fish, but it is on record that quite a number of stone wagons were in use earlier, hauled by horse-teams. The present steamer pier is a later structure, added in 1896. According to the *Dorset Year Book*, traffic from the pier comprised stone outwards and timber inwards by day, and coal by night.

The layout has changed at various times. About 1885 a large fish store was built half-way down the tramway, with a short branch entering it. It seems that bodies fished from the sea (and there were many wrecks hereabouts) also went down the tramway and part of the fish store was used as a morgue. An extant photograph of stone wagons standing in the short siding outside the fish store shows short four-wheeled wagons with outside journals, and no sides.

The tramway is still in place for about 100 yards from the fish store towards the pier; most is in flat-bottom rails of 30 ft lengths, but part is of tramway groove-rail. The pier itself has been allowed to decay, though still standing.

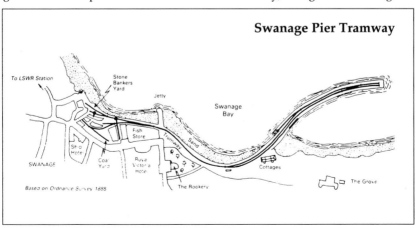

Swanage Pier Tramway

To LSWR Station • Stone Bankers Yard • Jetty • Swanage Bay • Fish Store • Tramway • Sand • Stn Hotel • SWANAGE • Coal Yard • Royal Victoria Hotel • Cottages • The Grove • Based on Ordnance Survey 1885 • The Rookery

The Swanage Pier Tramway in about 1890 at the passing loop before the pier entrance. The stone yard can be seen above the group of people at the left hand end of the jetty.

Frith, Reigate

This postcard of about 1906 shows two loaded stone wagons on the old pier, with the 1896 pier beyond.   *Stevens, Poole*

The Swanage Pier Tramway siding serving the fish store and coal yard as it was in 1973. Shops are on the site of the original stone yard.   *Author*

The Brownsea Island Tramway

In the early 1850s a somewhat fraudulent character, Col W.P. Waugh, thought he had discovered ball clay on Brownsea Island. He borrowed half-a-million pounds and proceeded to lay down equipment to work it: two potteries, a 200 ft drying shed, a substantial pier, coal pens, reservoir, and a narrow gauge railway serving these points and the mines which were mostly in the centre of the island. A company was formed, the Branksea Clay & Pottery Co. However, the clay turned out to be very poor; the Colonel had an extravagant life-style and profits were meagre. In 1857 he was made bankrupt, but working was carried on by the Trustees. In 1873 there were 240 people living on the island, but from 1877 the industry was run down. With some two miles of track, the railway might have used steam power, but there is no firm evidence to suggest this. According to one account, the person who sold the island to Col Waugh had 'salted' the quarry with real china clay.

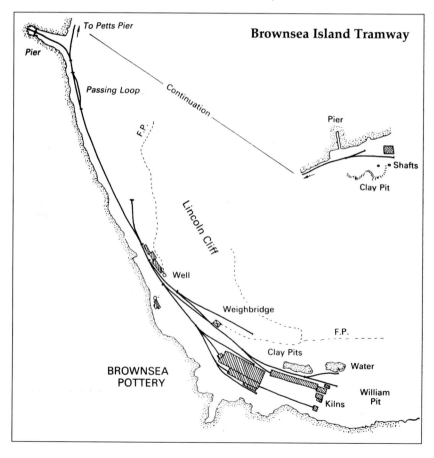

The Kimmeridge Shale Tramways

Interest in the shale deposits of Kimmeridge has lasted for nearly 2,000 years, and an oil rig was in 1970 pumping oil on almost the same spot as a Roman shale mine. The first use of railways here was probably about 1848, when an Act was obtained for 'constructing railways, inclines, causeways etc.', and the earliest line seems to be a short one from the cliffs at Yellow Ledge round the south side of the hill which is topped by Clavell's Tower (built 1837) to a level above the east shore of the bay. The line falls at a gradient of 1 in 40; nothing is known about it, but two lengths of heavy bridge-section rail lying in a gully at Gaulters Gap in the centre of the bay may have come from it, as also may a railway wheel being used as an anchor at the fishing 'hard'. This is 18 in. in diameter, cast-iron, with eight holes very similar to the wheels of wagons used to build the Plymouth breakwater about 1820. It has a pronounced flange on the inside and a small flange on the outside, and thus could not have been used on a railway having points of the normal type; this early Kimmeridge line is unlikely to have had any points and might have used only one wagon.

A longer line ran from a wooden pier at the east end of the bay past the coastguard cottages and then east to a shale pit (map ref. 916782) near the 'D Plantation' on the Smedmore Estate about half a mile from the bay, and then

This double-flanged wheel found by the author used as an anchor in Kimmeridge Bay could have come from the 1848 shale tramway, or possibly from the 1827 Portland Railway. *Author*

The trackbed of the 1848 tramway to the shale cliffs at Kimmeridge in May 1973, with Clavell's Tower beyond.   *Author*

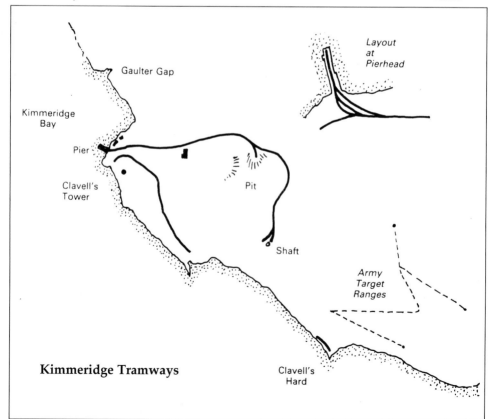

Kimmeridge Tramways

turning south, another half-mile to a shaft (map ref. 915787). A date of 1858 has been assigned to this, and it has been tied in with a company which processed shale oil at Wareham to supply lighting for Paris; but the large quantities of rail from it which still can be found, as a fence around Clavell's Tower, and on the 'hards' at the bay, suggest a later date. They are all flat-bottom, ranging in weights from about 15 lb./yd as might be found in workings, to some 30 lb./yd suited to the 'main line', and seem unlikely to have been rolled so early. The route at the bay end has been covered by tracks for holidaymakers, but inland the formation can be found if searched for carefully. A painting by Mr C. D'Oyly in Smedmore House shows the wooden pier *in situ* about 1900, and Sir Frederick Treves writing in 1906 stated that there were still wagons to be seen on the pier. Portions of four main supports for the pier can still be seen amongst the rocks.

The Bituminous Shale Company, who processed shale at Weymouth were active around 1850 and probably used the early line. Messrs Ferguson & Muschamp took over and moved the processing to Wareham, being only interested in turning the shale into fertiliser; there are no details of their method of transport. A French company under Marshall Pelissier was working the shale in the 1870s and is likely to have built the second line and the pier. The company was wound up in 1872, and no details have been found of any later use of the tramway.

A third tramway is thought to have existed on a working level half-way down the shale cliffs at Clavell's Hard, east of Kimmeridge Bay; there are tunnels here, and records of rails and iron ladders, together with iron sockets in the 'hard' itself which could have been used in connection with a telpher or incline to enable the shale to be loaded into barges.

Army Target Railways

During World War II the army laid down some railways for practising firing at moving targets, above the cliffs near Clavell's Hard; this was an ideal position as the shells would fall in the sea; a similar railway was laid on Seaford Head in Sussex. After the war the rails were lifted and the formation ploughed in.

The Cocknowle Tramway

A balance-worked railway incline is said to have been here 100 years ago; the site is almost certainly the formation of about 150 yds in length, barely perceptible amongst the gorse, which runs straight up the north face of Knowle Hill opposite a recently-opened chalk pit (map ref. 938821). What seems to be another railway, 200 yards long, runs from the foot of this incline on an easier gradient, to the west. This is slightly curved and could not have been balance-worked, but would have needed some sort of cable assistance. The object was the marl dug from pits at the top of the hill, and it was transported in carts to Ridge, where it was processed by the Wareham Cement Company at a premise close to that of Pike Brothers.

The bottom of the Cocknowle Tramway in a shallow cutting, May 1973.   *Author*

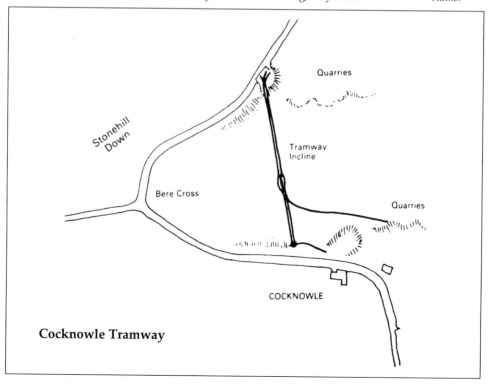

Cocknowle Tramway

Chapter Six

The New Swanage Railway

The idea of re-opening the Swanage branch was being actively canvassed even before it closed. British Rail moved with its usual indecent haste to take up the track; and mounting protest in August 1972 stopped them, by which time the only stretch which could be saved was about a quarter of a mile southwards from Furzebrook. The future did not look good; British Rail, giving the no doubt accurate picture that the last thing it wanted at Swanage was a railway, proposed to develop the station site. However, in the end it was sold to the Town Council for a car park - though the council was not totally opposed to the idea of a railway. Much patient lobbying ensued; in 1975 a local vote showed 83 per cent of the townspeople in favour of the railway. In the same year the Dorset County Council, which now owned the trackbed, apart from the Swanage station area, agreed to lease it to the new railway; but such was the unrealistic thinking that this was made contingent upon the Swanage Railway being able to run a service of at least four trains per day to Wareham by January 1980.

Plans continued to be made; it was decided to have stations at Herston, Harmans Cross, Corfe Castle, The Blue Pool (from where track was still in) and Worgret (just before the junction). The clay traffic was of course still running, though the oil problem had not yet arisen. BR was prepared to consider its own staff taking trains on from Blue Pool to Wareham. However, there was still another hurdle; the authorities wanted to use the trackbed through the gap at Corfe for a by-pass.

Some stock was purchased: the 4-wheel Planet diesel locomotive *Beryl* from Hamworthy coal wharf, an ex-SR class '4', 2-6-4T No. 80078, and an ex-SR utility van No. 1234, later No. DS3065. These were placed in the old goods shed. The body of an ex-LSWR 6-wheel 6-compartment Third class carriage No. 695 was obtained, placed on the cattle dock at Corfe, and restored to the LSWR pinkish livery. At Swanage a short length of track was laid alongside the station platform but shortly afterwards moved to the old coaling platform and scenery van 4594 put there for painting. In 1977 some further track was lifted from Eldon's Sidings, where it had been the property of the clay company and not of BR, and in 1978 an ex-GWR hand-crane which had been purchased two years earlier arrived. By now a Bulleid corridor coach No. 4365 had come from WD Long Marston (Army 5200), and was placed in the goods shed for extensive restoration. More motive power came: ex-GWR 0-6-2T No. 6695 (not in working order), a Fowler 1957 0-4-0DM *May* from the Ministry of Works in Manchester, and *Richard Trevithick*, an 0-4-0ST Barclay (1954) from Godrington power station. There was a small victory on 28th August, 1979 when it was possible to announce a diesel-hauled train service, but only as far as the Northbrook Road bridge. The railway's ex-SR Bulleid Brake Third was followed by Maunsell Third Open No. 1381, and in 1981 another Third Brake No. 2768. Herston loop was laid.

Progress at Swanage by 20th October, 1978; the 2-6-4T No. 80078 has been stripped, and GWR 0-6-2T No. 6695 has arrived. The short section of track from the engine shed area is ex-London Transport. *Author*

Swanage station in July 1985. Ex-Midland railway 0-6-0T No. 41708 on loan from Butterley is backing onto two coaches from the SR Bulleid Set 298. *A.K. Pfrangley*

Observers would have felt that success was very unlikely. However, perseverance had its reward. For the 1982 season a service was run for one mile to Herston – a short wooden platform with Portakabin attachment. The service was worked by a Hawthorn, Leslie 0-6-0ST built in 1938. Harmans Cross (3 miles) was forecast for 1983, but this could not be achieved, partly due to the necessity to rebuild Knitson bridge. More rolling stock arrived; perhaps one of the most noteworthy was de-motored ' Brighton Belle' Pullman motor-coach No. S288, transferred in 1982 to Swanage from the Stour Valley Preservation Society, later passed on to the Venice Simplon Orient Express train operator.

A vital event on 24th July, 1986 was the vote by the County Council not to use the former railway through Corfe for a new road.

The society had support from other private railways; its first services were worked by a 'B4' 0-4-0T of the Bluebell Railway. Later famous engines such as *Flying Scotsman* and SR 'S15' class 4-6-0 No. E828 appeared. Passenger stock was somewhat mixed, but was improved by the acquisition of a 2-coach dmu from the North Yorkshire Moors Railway (later joined by a four-motor one) and some BR Mk I carriages.

When Harmans Cross station was opened in March 1989 it had only one platform, but in 1996 a second was added, and a signal box, which allowed more frequent trains at peak times. A lease was obtained in 1987 for the track as far as the BR boundary at Furzebrook, and a Light Railway Order obtained to Norden.

There was a financial crisis in 1991 but it was overcome and trains ran to Corfe and Norden from 12th August, 1995, though the official openings were in February 1996. Norden station is almost on the site of the former Eldon Sidings, north of Slepe Road bridge, and has a pathway to a large park and ride car park off the Wareham-Corfe road. In 1997 32,037 passengers used the station, and 19,651 used the park and ride.

Engines regularly used were 'M7' class 0-4-4T No. 30053 (which returned in 1984 from the USA), BR Standard 2-6-4T No. 80104, Bulleid Pacific No. 34072 *257 Squadron* and ex-Midland Railway 0-6-0T No. 41708. A large repair facility was set up in a 9,000 sq. ft former cosmetics factory near Herston, and USA tank No. 30075, GWR 0-6-2T No. 6695 and others are receiving attention there. A replacement 50 ft turntable for Swanage was obtained from Neasden. BR Standard 2-6-4T No. 80078 went into service in November 1999, 23 years after it had been acquired!

The following carriages have worked on the railway, many on loan (building dates given where known):

SR Third Open No. 1381 (1931)
SR Passenger Brake No. 2768
SR Passenger Brake (1941)
SR Open Third No. 4365 (1947)
SR Open Third No. 4366 (1947)
SR Corridor Composite No. 5761 (1947)
SR Open Second No. 4416 (1956)
SR Open Second No. 4349 (1956

LMS Third Open No. 7868 (1925)

BR Corridor Second No. 18424 (1957)
BR Restaurant Coach No. 1908 (1957)
BR Second Sleeper No. 2564 (1958)
BR Brake Composite No. 21205 (1958)

Pullman No. 335, on loan from SLOA 1995
Pullman Motor Third No. 288 (1932)

Herston Halt in July 1985 with 0-6-0ST No. 21 having arrived on a two-coach train from Swanage.   *A.K. Pfrangley*

BR Standard 2-6-4T No. 80104 is seen approaching Harmans Cross with the 11.50 Swanage-Norden train on 14th August, 1997.   *J. Scrace*

A Swanage train leaving Harmans Cross in July 1997, after the passing loop had been installed; the 'M7' class 0-4-4T is No. 30053. *J. Scrace*

The Swanage Railway's 'M7' 0-4-4T No. 30053 entering Swanage; the scene is little changed from LSWR days apart from the double doors to the shed and the clock (which shows it is the 13.10 departure from Norden) on 28th July, 1997. *J. Scrace*

Little changed from LSWR days: Swanage station on 30th July, 1999, with miscellaneous stock in the bay and passengers waiting for the Norden train. At the buffers far left is Pacific 34028 *Eddystone* awaiting completion of restoration.   R.A.W. Kidner

In recent years reliance has been placed in Mk I stock of the former British Rail, including TSOs Nos. 4842, 4961, 4349, 4981/3 and First Open No. 3090. Two RU(K) vehicles, Nos. 1937 and 81146, are being restored for a Dining Train.

In 1999 it was necessary to borrow LNER 'N7' class class 0-6-2T No. 7999 to ensure the intense headway in the high season; however Bulleid Pacific No. 34072 *257 Squadron* returned in May from an overhaul at the Herston Works of Southern Locomotives Ltd and '4MT' 2-6-4T No. 80104 and 'S15 class' 4-6-0 No. E828 were also in traffic.

At the end of the year track was being laid northwards from Norden and had reached the site of the former Eldon Siding.

For the millennium season, the railway has taken a lease of a class '33' diesel of a type familiar to the locality, No. 33 012. 'M7' tank No. 30053 also remains on lease until 2001.

A stranger in Purbeck: ex-LNER 0-6-2T No. 7999 was hired in 1999 to maintain increased services on the Swanage Railway.   R.A.W. Kidner

Appendix One

Southern Steam Trust Stock 1999

Coaches

Coach BCK 21205
Bulleid Coach BTSO 4365
Coach SK W18424
Coach Mk I TSO 4074
Coach Mk I 4055, Royal Wessex Bar Car
Coach DS 70011 TK 728, Ironclad
Coach BSOB 9015
Coach SO 4803
Coach FO 3090
Share in Maunsell Coach BDT 6699
Coach SKH 24127
Bulleid SO No. 1457
Coach RU 1937 Kitchen Car
Coach BG 81146
Coach Mk I BSK 35464
Coach Mk I TSO 4961
Bulleid Coach BTSO 4366
Coack Mk I TSO 4349
Coach TSO 4983

Vans and Wagons

Scenery Van 4594
Dolphin Flat Wagon 274569
Dogfish Wagon DB992784
Crane CB5968
Crane CC1101
Crane ADS50286
Match Wagon ADB 50286
PMV 1628

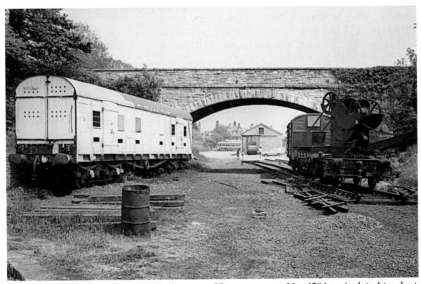

Early days of the new Swanage Railway: ex-SR scenery van No. 4594 on isolated track at the former coaling stage. The hand crane and ex-SR Utility No. 1234 were the only other vehicles there on 31st May, 1978. *Author*

Appendix Two

Recent Middlebere Track Studies

Mr M. Wilmott has given permission for a brief report on his recent study of remaining relics at Middlebere, calling for some excavation. He found that the peg holes in stone sleepers were from 44 in. to 46 in. apart. The sleepers measured 12-15 in. long by 14-19 in. wide, and 4-6 in. deep. Grooves worn by the plates were 5-5½ in.; the gauge may have been as narrow as 3 ft 6 in. Portions of rail showed side measurements of 3 in.

He also found at the wharf an area where blocks were at 5 ft spacing instead of 3 ft, suggesting that some structure, possibly for mending broken 'balls', had been there. He also examined the track bed between the former smithy and Eldon's Siding and found no evidence of stone blocks having been present; it seems probable that this portion of the line was edge rail at times.

Mr Wilmott was also responsible for persuading the Secretary of State to 'list' three items: the two tunnels at Norden and the engine shed at Ridge.

Mr M. Lewis, who did some similar work in 1968, donated a section of plate to the Ironbridge Gorge Museum.

Acknowledgements

I would like to thank the many people who have assisted in elucidating the facts included in this book, and especially: Mr L. Popplewell, Swanage Library, the Dorset County Library, Mr R. Wear, Mr D. Gould, Mr R. Roberts, Swanage UDC Engineer, Major J. Mansell of Smedmore House, Mr S.M. Barrell, Mr D. Faulkner, Mr G. Brigden, M. Wilmott, B. March and the Swanage Railway.

Bibliography

The following have been consulted:

Pike Bros, Fayle & Co. Ltd by W.J.K. Davies (Narrow Gauge Railway Society Handbook No. 1)
The Middlebere Tramway by B. Baxter (Railway & Canal Historical Society)
Brownsea's Lost Railway by L. Popplewell (Dorset Yearbook)
Purbeck Island by R. Legg
Unknown Dorset by D. Maxwell
Inventory of Historical Monuments in the County of Dorset (Vol. 1 S.E.)
Stephen Lewin and the Poole Foundry by R. Wear & E. Lees (Industrial Railway Society)
The Railway Magazine
The Southern Railway Magazine